PUNGO TALES FOUR: THEN AND NOW

by

Walter A. Whitehurst

An original compilation of tales by the author and others
(Everyone who has told me stories included in this book has given me verbal or written permission to publish them.)

Published by

HEADLIGHT PRESS
6500 Clito Road
Statesboro, Georgia 30461

© 2014 by Walter A. Whitehurst
ALL RIGHTS RESERVED!
Cover Art by Fred Havens

ISBN: 1-58535-267-5

Dedication

It is my pleasure to dedicate this book to the memory of my parents, John Walter Whitehurst and Elsie Mae Williams Whitehurst. I was born during the Great Depression, which was a very difficult time, and Dad's health was not good, due to a kidney stone operation that kept him in the hospital for twelve weeks. Mother often said that we would have been better off if his health had been better. They sacrificed a great deal to provide for my two sisters and me. I am very grateful for what our parents did for us.

About the Cover

Where the nice high Pungo Ferry Bridge crossing the North Landing River is located, there used to be a ferry. (Yes, there actually was a ferry.) As a child I remember that ferry, which took up to four cars across the water. Attached to the ferry was a boat (like a small tugboat) which pushed the ferry across and then turned around and pushed it back. I can picture on that boat a FORD logo like the one we see today on cars and trucks.

Donavan Bonney, who lived very near the ferry, said his first summer job was on the ferry. He also said that Mac Carroll, the pilot of the boat, had two thumbs on each hand. I wondered if that was one of the requirements to drive that boat.

The bridge in the picture replaced the ferry in the late 1940's. Many years later, Fred Havens took the picture of the bridge on the very day they were beginning to demolish that first bridge in order to build the present high-rise bridge. Thanks to Fred for sharing this picture.

TABLE OF CONTENTS

FOREWORD

I. PUNGO PERSONALITIES—PAST
  The Life of Napoleon Bonaparte Capps 11
  Theophilus Bartee ("Uncle Bill") 13
  Don Wright, an Outstanding Carpenter 17
  Leon Thompson, a Fine Mechanic 20
  Lucy Murden, a Pungo Matriarch 23

II. PUNGO PERSONALITIES – PRESENT
  Allie the Deer Hunter 27
  Bill Dixon: From Deer Hunter to Deer Healer 31
  Roy Flanagan, Extension Agent 36
  Jack Fentress, Game Warden / Airplane Pilot 40
  Kermit Mitchell, Wedding Magistrate 44
  Rita Joyner and the Silver Tappers 47

III. PUNGO -- PAST AND PRESENT
  "Tribes," A Movie Made in Pungo 51
  A Tale of Two Ponies 56
  "Whatever Happened To . . . ?" 59
  The Pungo Ridge Winery 66
  The "Creature" at Charity Preschool 68
  Pungo Goes Global 72

IV. SOME SPECIAL PUNGO EVENTS
  The Moving of the Barbershop ... and More 77
  The Lost Pictures 82
  A Very Special Wedding 84
  The Witches of Pungo Celebrate Halloween 87
  The Witch of Pungo, 2013 92
  A Tribute to Five Brave Surfmen 94

V. **IN THEIR OWN WORDS**
The Remarkable Jones Family
  Letters from Estelle Jones Bowers 99
A Man Close to God: Lonnie Lee Murphy, 1898-1995
  By Terry Gregory 103
My Pets
  By Beth Swanner 105
Growing Older Is Part of God's Plan
  A poem by Beth Swanner... 108

Foreword

One of the many things I enjoyed about being a local church pastor was visiting in people's homes. I would look at the pictures they had hanging on their walls, the style of their house, their furniture, etc. It would help me know what was important in their lives.

In our conversation I'd ask where they were from, what their work was, if they had children, and if they were involved in church. During the course of our conversation, I got to know the families quite well. It has always been a joy for me to meet new people.

That is precisely what happens when I visit with people for them to tell me their stories for the *Pungo Tales* books. It has been a joy to get to know new persons and to learn more about friends I have known for many years. Indeed, Pungo has some wonderful people.

Another thing I enjoy is telling stories. Our son Bruce is President and CEO of the Virginia Bankers Association, which publishes a bimonthly magazine, "Virginia Banking," and in each edition Bruce writes an article titled "Insights." In the January/February 2014 issue he wrote, "My dad has always loved to tell stories, which served him well as a missionary and United Methodist Minister. . . . [He] has written three books full of stories about Pungo, the quaint and still somewhat rural area of Virginia Beach near Sandbridge . . . . In a quick Internet search near the end of last year about 2014 trends, storytelling showed up in several places as a top marketing trend." Bruce went on to suggest that banks need to tell their stories in their communities.

Again, I want to thank my wife Betty for editing this book and my daughter Mónica for proofreading it, as they have done with previous books. Writing these books has given me the opportunity to tell many stories that can be read over and over. I hope the readers will enjoy reading these tales as much as I have enjoyed writing them.

-- *Walt Whitehurst, Pungo, March 2014*

I.

PUNGO

PERSONALITIES –

PAST

THE LIFE OF NAPOLEON BONAPARTE CAPPS
(As told by Mike Newbill)

Napoleon Bonaparte Capps was born around 1837 and died in 1861 at approximately 24 years of age. He was the great-great-grandfather of Mike Newbill, who has done extensive research on him. Napoleon's family thought that he reached the rank of captain in the Confederate Army, but it is now believed that he was a private with the Princess Anne Calvary, 5th Virginia Calvary. *(According to Kenneth Harris, in* Princess Anne County, Virginia: Its Contributions and Sacrifices to the War Between the States, *p. 127. Capps enlisted at Cape Henry on April 20, 1861, and left his company on July 8, 1861, to return to Princess Anne County.)* It is believed that he may have the ill-fated distinction of serving the shortest time of anybody from Princess Anne County. Family tradition is that he died of pneumonia immediately after returning home.

Mike said, "I found four deeds of properties that Napoleon Bonaparte Capps bought or sold in the Pungo and/or Creeds area. I haven't been able to pin down the location of those properties. I think he was reasonably wealthy for those times, buying and selling properties, owning slaves, etc. I have been trying to find out where he lived since that may be where his grave is. Also, there is no record of his death or marriage that I can find. I think his wife was Sarah Oakham, and I have wondered if possibly he and Sarah were in a common law marriage.

"Another family tradition is that Napoleon's wife ran off to New York with a Yankee officer, leaving two small children. As we know, family tradition is often suspect; who knows, maybe it did happen. And maybe he died of a broken heart rather than disease (a romantic speculation). The traitorous wife supposedly had a daughter by her Yankee who became one of the first female attorneys in California, most likely in the 1880's or 90's. Sometimes the stories are better than reality, but often they are trumped by reality. Again, who knows in this case?"

Napoleon's daughter Rosa Capps, Mike's great-grandmother, was born on March 26, 1861, and died on August 14, 1933. Her grandmother Oakham raised her after her mother went to New York. She was married and widowed twice at a relatively young age, and then lived in Norfolk with a daughter, Mike's great-aunt, for many years.

Mike's grandmother and great-aunt seldom mentioned Napoleon or Rosa, causing him to think there might have been some issues about the Capps side of the family that they kept secret. Rosa is buried in Forest Lawn Cemetery in Norfolk. Napoleon's burial site remains a mystery.

If you study genealogy, you may find that the name Napoleon Bonaparte was very popular in those years. Perhaps with our Napoleon Bonaparte Capps' sadness at not being faithful as a soldier and losing his wife and his life at an early age, he may have been somewhat like another Napoleon who met his Waterloo!

THEOPHILUS BARTEE ("UNCLE BILL")

Theophilus Bartee was my great-uncle. He was a brother of my grandmother, Sallie Elizabeth Bartee Williams. We called him "Uncle Bill," maybe because Theophilus was hard to pronounce. It's not a name you hear every day, although it appears twice in the New Testament, in Luke 1:3 and Acts 1:1. The meaning of the name is "One who loves God." I remember the boathouse he had beside the larger West Neck Creek Bridge, across from what is now the West Neck Marina. His house was somewhat close to the bridge. He had rowboats that he rented to people who wanted to go fishing in West Neck Creek. I often went there to rent a boat, not so much to fish, but just to go around with my cousin Gene Whitehurst and explore the little areas that branched out from the creek. Those are good memories.

I told my cousin Goldie Bartee that I remembered Uncle Bill as a quiet, gentle person, and she said, "Yes, that is true. He didn't talk much unless he had a drink of liquor. Then he rambled on and on. In fact, that's the way all the Bartees were." Goldie continued, "My husband Herman went to see Uncle Bill after his wife Rosa died. He told Herman that he had buried some money out in the back yard. Herman told Uncle Bill to tell his son Willie about it. Later Herman asked Willie if his father had told him about the money and Willlie said "yes."

I telephoned Willie's son Billy and asked him if Willie ever found that money. He said "yes," although I have the impression that Billy himself never got any of that money. Also Billy said, "In the old house they found $87.00 under the rug in the middle of the front room. And they found Rosa's money in her books – ten- and twenty-dollar bills hidden in several of the books on her bookshelf."

It is a pleasure to share the following poems written about Uncle Bill. The first one was written by Elliott Jones, with permission to publish it given by Elliott's widow, Edith Jones (a niece of Goldie Bartee).

Mr. Thee's Boathouse

Mr. Thee,
Well, the older ones
Called him that.
To me,
He was Mr. Bartee.
Still others said he was
Three Apples and a Bottle of Tea;
Theophilus was his name.
When he was young he farmed
The high land near the river.
When he was older,
He began renting rowboats,
Oars, fishing poles for quarters,
Half dollars, change.
Little skiffs, old oars,
Rattling locks
From the rickety dock
Low to the water level –
Boats no more than
Twelve inches high at the side,
Old, old boats
Nailed juniper
Swelled water tight
Sunken and then bailed,
No glue – no paint.
All mostly for quiet contentment.
He had, I guess, a half dozen
Or no more than eight
Craft. His old chair on
The dock planks . . . .

I remember a pipe,
And his quiet eye,
His gentle voice,
And his gentle business;
Gently, something remains,
Nicer than juniper wood
And blue creek water
In the morning.

-- Elliott Jones

- - - - - - -

In 1968, Jack Bartee, a retired United Methodist pastor and a nephew of Uncle Bill, wrote the following poem. Permission to publish it was given by his widow, Anne Bartee.

Uncle Bill Is Gone

Old Uncle Bill is gone.
We knew his end was coming soon –
But still the news shocked us a little.

And who was old Uncle Bill?
Daddy knew him – but I didn't.
To me he was just an old guy with funny shoes.
(Funny I should remember mainly the shoes!)

I saw old Uncle Bill just two or three times:
In particular I remember that warm April afternoon
When Daddy and I visited him under his front yard
    shade-tree.
That was when the funny shoes became etched in my
    memory.

I was too young then to know the person wearing those
    funny shoes:
Who put them on dawn after dawn just after getting out of
    bed,

Who drove his little English Ford in them to West Neck
   Creek at mid-morning (he looked after a boat-rental
   house there),
Who propped the shoes up against a pier railing as he sat
   remembering in the Virginia mid-day sun,
And who took them off wearily by his bedside at night after
   the boats were all in.

Shoes don't make a man, of course.
(Not even funny shoes!)
But of all that Uncle Bill was –
The brain, heart, skin, and hormones,
His hopes, loves and needs,
Eighty-plus years of days and nights –
All I remember, or ever really knew, is the funny shoes.
Funny I should remember those doggone shoes . . . .

Who was the person called "Uncle Bill"?
Who, for that matter, is the person that is I?
And what shoes shall I be remembered by, when what is me
   is gone?

— Jack Bartee

That's an interesting thought

for each of us to consider.

DON WRIGHT, AN OUTSTANDING CARPENTER
(As told by his widow Jenny and his son Dennis)

I met Jenny Wright in the waiting room of Pungo's dentist, Dr. Bek, and after she realized that I am the author of the "Pungo Tales" books, we had a delightful conversation. When she asked if I had met her husband Don, I had to say "no." She went on to say that my dad knew Don and that he had done some carpenter work for Dad and for many people in Pungo. After she left, it occurred to me that it would be interesting to include Don's story in this book. I had failed to get Jenny's phone number, but later when I interviewed Polly Thompson about her husband Leon, she told me that Jenny is her sister. Immediately I asked for Jenny's phone number. With that I arranged to meet with Jenny and her son Dennis.

Jenny came from Covington to live in Virginia Beach in 1952, and her sister Polly moved here shortly after that. Jenny worked for the Vocational Technical School on North Landing Road for 38 years. Don was from Sand Point, Idaho, and he retired from the military and remained here. He and Jenny met through a friend and were married when she was 16 years old and he was 21.

Dennis remembers that Don made an addition to my parents' house as well as putting a new roof on the house. In each house he built, he also made a bench that had a hinged seat which covered a large, convenient storage area. (The bench he built for my parents' house is still in my home.)

When Don and Dennis learned that my dad loved to make turtle soup, they caught a turtle and took it to Dad so he could make a pot of turtle soup. When Dennis was asked if he enjoyed the soup, he said, "a little bit" (which sounded somewhat close to "no"). He does remember that there were several different kinds of meat in a turtle. Even though my dad was a good cook, his turtle soup was not among my favorites either.

Don built the parsonage for Tabernacle United Methodist Church. He built several houses at the Virginia Beach waterfront, and unfortunately he lost his tools during the Ash Wednesday storm in 1962. He also built the house of Frank Williams in Back Bay and the one beside Charity United Methodist Church where Doris Baker lives today. He built Jack Shell's house on Princess Anne Road, seven houses on Seaboard Road, and one on Knotts Island. He designed these houses according to what the people wanted, at no extra cost. "People often said that he was the best builder in Virginia Beach," Jenny said.

Even though he was the owner of the construction company, Don paid himself the exact same salary he paid his workers. That's just the type of person he was. One time he fell off a roof and broke an ankle, but that didn't slow him down for long. He was very intelligent, and he did a little bit of everything. He never slowed down to teach Dennis anything about building. Also, he did have an alcohol problem, although he knew when he had drunk too much and he did not go to work on those days.

At one time, George Wilson took Jenny to clean houses at Sandbridge Beach. One house she cleaned was that of the Corbitts. When Mrs. Corbitt died, she left to Jenny her house and a Cadillac car. Jenny lived there a few years, but later she sold the house and the car and moved to her present house – one that Don had built, originally for someone else.

Dennis remembers that his dad made his first duck decoy for him. In fact, Dennis has a burlap bag full of decoys Don made. In addition to duck hunting, he and his dad also did other hunting. In 1967, Dennis killed his first deer in Pungo. He even saw a bear on the former property of Joe Burroughs on Seaboard Road where there is now a golf course.

In his later years, before he died in 1993, Don started raising rabbits. One time he had as many as 300 rabbits. This was not a fundraising project. He gave them away and was delighted to do that. Jenny and Dennis remember Don as a down-to-earth type of person. I could tell from our conversation that I would really have enjoyed knowing him.

LEON THOMPSON, A FINE MECHANIC
(As told by his widow, Polly Thompson)

Leon Thompson was an excellent mechanic. He ran a Gulf service station on Laskin Road and later had other stations on Virginia Beach Boulevard before working at R.K. Chevrolet and then at Brud Buick in Norfolk. His last job was with English Construction Company. Even though Leon had been dead for a year and a half when I interviewed Polly, that company was still sending Christmas gifts to his home.

As we sat on Polly's nice front porch, I asked her to tell me about Leon. She started off by saying, "I remember hearing him tell me many times about what happened when he was a boy. At that time they were living in a house behind Bethel Church of God on Indian River Road, and Leon got his tail beaten for going where he wasn't supposed to go. I think he learned a lesson from that experience." (She did not tell me where he went.) Later his dad built their house on North Muddy Creek Road where the family lived for many years.

I asked when she met Leon, and she said that it was in 1954 when she moved here from West Virginia to be near her sister, Jenny Wright. Polly went to the Grand Ole Opry at Hampton Coliseum and Leon was there. I asked if it was love at first sight, and she said "not exactly, but we both loved country music and bowling, and gradually we started dating."

Polly worked as a custodian at the Vocational Technical School on North Landing Road for 32 years. She remembers that during that time a new church rented that building for Sunday morning services. One of her special responsibilities was to leave everything nice and clean on Friday for the church to use, as well as leaving unlocked the doors they would need. She later substituted at the Three

Oaks Elementary School, located near the intersection of Princess Anne Road and Sandbridge Road.

One house they lived in was on the property in Pungo where Sherwood Lakes is now located. Polly said that house stood exactly where the middle of the larger lake is now. It's hard to imagine that there was ever a house there.

Thirty years ago Leon and Polly purchased the house and three acres of land where she still lives. She laughed and said, "Leon always wanted to have a lot of land. I preferred something smaller, but he won out on the decision. But the funny thing about that is that he did not even see the place before we bought it. He asked our daughter Vicky to look at the place and she liked it so he bought it." The problem is that Polly has been left with the job of mowing all that land. Not that she doesn't like to mow, but she would have preferred a smaller lot. When she goes to the cemetery, she stands over his grave and fusses at him for leaving her with such a big job to do. Nevertheless, she does good work in taking care of it. It is a beautiful place.

Leon was not necessarily a people person. Polly is just the opposite. She likes to be with people and enjoys being friendly with others. Leon did not like noise. He was generally a quiet person, although when he was unhappy with something a person said or did, he could express very strongly his reaction to that. Whenever a person came into the house, he expected that person to speak to him first and then he would return the greeting. Whenever Leon's niece Beth Thompson came to visit, she always wanted to give Leon a hug, but he did not like that. However, later in life after he became ill with Alzheimer's, Beth would ask if she could hug him and he would open his arms and say, "Yes, of course!"

Another thing about Leon in his latter days was that he liked to make fires. For example, he set fire to stumps and enjoyed watching them burn. His love for setting fires is what led to his death. Polly forgot to take his cigarette lighter away from him that day, and while he was in the bathroom he set his shirt on fire. He came running out of the bathroom and ran to the porch. She poured water on him and put the fire out, but he had already burned the upper part of his body. Polly called 911 and the helicopter came to take him to the hospital. Ironically, one thing Leon always said was, "I'll never fly in an airplane!" He never did fly except when he didn't know what he was doing. Maybe the lesson from that is to be careful when we name something that we will never do!

LUCY W. MURDEN, A PUNGO MATRIARCH
(As told by her son, Lloyd A. "Buddy" Murden, Jr.)

Lucy Murden, 92, died on January 7, 2013, and I went to her funeral, which was a celebration of her life. I was so impressed with her life that I asked her son, Lloyd Murden, Jr., to meet with me and share his impressions to include in this book.

Lucy and Lloyd Sr. had three children: Joyce Newman, Barbara Henley, and Lloyd Jr. Lucy was the homemaker, which meant that she stayed home and took care of the children and was an excellent cook. Buddy (Lloyd Jr.'s nickname) soon learned that lunch was ready exactly at 12:00 and he had to be punctual in order to eat. If he got there as late as 12:15, she had already put the food away. That tradition has stayed with him throughout his life. When I telephoned his wife Barbara around 11:00 a.m. about setting up an appointment with him for an interview, she said that he wasn't there but he would be there at 12:00 for his home-cooked meal. Some things from our childhood stay with us. When I called Buddy at 12:15, I asked him if he had finished lunch, to which he said "yes."

For many years, Lucy's husband ran Murden's Store at the corner of Princess Anne Road and Pleasant Ridge Road. During much of that time their cousin Emily Capps worked at the store. But Emily left the store to pursue other goals in her life, and since Buddy was in school, Lucy started working in the store from late morning until mid-afternoon while her husband went home to work in the garden. The Pleasant Ridge Post Office was located in that store, with Lloyd Sr. as Postmaster and Lucy as Postmistress. Sometimes a person who could not read or write would ask her to fill out some paperwork. In those days it didn't matter that it was prohibited for postal employees to fill out papers for clients. She really enjoyed helping them. She liked greeting people and getting to know them. She was definitely a people person. Buddy said, "She knew everybody from Dam Neck to Knotts Island, but gradually new people started moving into Princess Anne County and Lucy greeted them just as warmly as the ones she knew."

She was very active at Charity United Methodist Church, and served for many years as treasurer of the United Methodist Women. The members of that group remember her with much affection and appreciation. She loved children very much and it is remembered how she made special cookies for them with a hole in the middle, and they liked putting their fingers through the cookies.

Lucy's birthday was on December 25, and she was very happy to share her birthday with Jesus. She was gypped out of birthday presents, but that was no problem for her. Quilting was her specialty and she spent endless hours making quilts. People would bring patches to her and she'd put them together, by hand. They would ask her why not sew them together with a sewing machine, but she thought it should be done the old-fashioned way.

Buddy regrets not listening to her more, and not asking her questions about people and events. She knew so many people and who was related to whom. Often we look back after a parent or other loved one has passed away and wish we had gotten more information from them.

I asked Buddy if there was some funny thing about her he'd like to share. He mentioned that she had dementia in her later years and generally her memory was not good. However, on many occasions he would ask her to name in order all 16 children in the Bright family to which she was related.

Usually she came up with all or just about all of them, which amazed those who heard her do it. It is an honor to include her in this book.

II.

PUNGO

PERSONALITIES –

PRESENT

ALLIE THE DEER HUNTER
(As told by Allie Irving and her mother Amy)

Tiffany Bright, a friend of the Irving family, shared on Facebook what Amy Irving had written: "The first time Allie went hunting, she killed two does. The second time hunting, she killed a nine-pointer. I can't imagine what she is going to kill the next time." Who were they talking about here? They were talking about Allie Irving, the nine-year-old daughter of Rick and Amy Irving and granddaughter of David and Susan Flanagan.

When Allie was asked if what Tiffany wrote was true, she said "Yes." She went on to explain that the first time she hunted deer on the Eastern Shore was September 28, 2013. That was "Youth Hunting Day" when only youth were allowed to shoot deer. On that day adults must accompany the youth but are not permitted to shoot. The youth must carry their own guns, although Allie's dad flipped off the safety and covered one of her eyes so she could sight the deer. Two other youth were there with them, and Rick's friend's son Dalton shot two does and Allie shot two, but they only found three of them. The fourth doe ran off into the marsh. They searched for an hour but never found her.

It was on Allie's second deer hunt with her dad on November 16, 2013, that she shot and killed the nine-pointer. Allie had always wanted to hunt, but never could do it before because she was too young. Youth hunting begins the year a person turns nine years old, and Allie's ninth birthday was in December 2013. She said, "I used to not be able to hunt because I had volleyball on Saturday and church on Sunday. Today (Saturday, November 23, 2013) I have to go to a birthday party and can't go hunting." When asked whether she would prefer to go to a party or hunting, Allie replied, "Hunting!"

Allie's dad Rick does a lot of hunting – "We're buddies," Allie says. Amy adds, "Sometimes I come home from teaching and find Allie and her four-year-old sister Emmie in the 'man room' above the garage, where Rick has all his hunting trophies and paraphernalia. They love to spend time there." Emmie "shoots" at deer on the TV, like Allie used to do when she was three or four years old. Amy said, "I'm the only one in the family that doesn't hunt, but maybe I'll try some day." Allie quickly exclaimed, "I'll carry the gun for you, Mom!"

When asked "What's it like to kill a deer?" Allie says, "It's really exciting! When you first see a deer, when one pops out, you just want to shoot right away." When asked if she eats the deer, her response was, "Yes, my dad cleans and cooks it. And not only that, I'm going to have it mounted and put it on the wall. It will be put on my bedroom wall in March. It costs about $275.00 to mount. They have to get the insides of the head out and put heavy foam inside."

Being a part of the Flanagan family that has raised turkeys for several generations, Allie likes to stay home from school the day of turkey killing to help pluck and dress the turkeys and pull the wagon. Her Aunt Ann Gregory taught her to dress turkeys, and she was the youngest dresser at turkey killing until her cousin Avonlea began to help dress turkeys in November 2013. Amy quickly added that Allie has to make good grades on her report card in order to stay home from school. That is a big incentive for her. And of course, Emmie wants to stay home from preschool and help, too, but she is not the youngest helper. Her younger cousin Lucas Flanagan sometimes helps.

When Allie was asked if she likes school, she said, "Sometimes!" Then came another question for Allie: "What's it like growing up in Pungo?" Her first response was that it is kind of hard growing up with a bunch of boys around, referring to her cousins who live next door. Her cousins are Colby, Bailey, Fletcher, and Lucas Flanagan, along with their sister Avonlea. Then Allie went on to say it is not a very busy life. She likes living close to Grandma and Grandpa.

It means a great deal to Allie to be a part of the 4-H Club, which for many local youth means the opportunity to raise an animal. She has not raised one yet, but her plans for next year include raising two pigs, although her mother thinks that one would be enough. She likes being able to go outdoors whenever she wants to -- there is plenty of land to play on -- and enjoys seeing the bright stars at night. Finally, there was a big smile on her face when she said, "I'm beginning to learn to drive the tractor." Next she was asked what she wants to be when she grows up. You may have already guessed that her response was "A veterinarian!"

Allie's first hunting experience was when she was six or seven years old and went rabbit hunting with her dad. She did not shoot the rabbits, but she watched out for them. Her gun's name is Roxie. Rick says every gun should have a name. His gun is Sally. Allie said, "Daddy even names his deer heads."

When a photo of Allie and the deer she had shot was emailed to her Uncle Roy Flanagan and his wife Jeannie, their 13-year-old son Colby responded by sending her a photo of a squirrel he had shot, saying, "You're not the only one in the family that can kill things!"

(See Photo on Following Page)

Allie and Rick Irving with Allie's deer
(Photo provided by Allie Irving)

BILL DIXON: FROM DEER HUNTER TO DEER HEALER

An article about Bill Dixon titled "A Deer Hunter Turned Healer" in the Norfolk Virginian Pilot, *August 3, 2013, tells about how he discovered orphaned baby deer whose mothers "had been killed by bobcats, coyotes, or, most often, by cars," and saved their lives by feeding and protecting them. I was so impressed by this very interesting story that I decided to have an interview with Bill to include in this book.*

Bill started off by telling about his Christian faith. He said that as we relate to God, it's not so much our ability but God's unlimited possibilities. He says, "Lord, you let me know how we are going to accomplish your will for me." After he made a commitment to God, he learned not to worry so much about things. He has had a lot of great adventures in life, but in these last ten to twelve years he has had no need to worry. His work is selling boats, a business that has not been too good in recent years. That means he doesn't have a steady monthly income. Some days all things go well just as he has planned; when they do not, he tries to make the best of it. He has learned:
    …to bloom where he is planted.
    …that God never lets him get bored.
    …that the trip is where the joy is.

For Bill, feeding the deer is a divine element. His dad, Frank, loved the Lord and he loved to hunt. He was a professional photographer who for many years took pictures for black high schools. With those schools he never had to sign a contract. It was a matter of a handshake. But after integration, in dealing with schools run by white administrators a contract was always required.

Bill's dad taught him to love to hunt and to respect whitetail deer. They especially went hunting during the Thanksgiving season. He also taught Bill not to waste any part of the animal and to thank the Lord for the bounty of hunting for the sustenance of the body. He believed that God put deer here for us to eat and to benefit the soul.

When his dad died, Bill gave the eulogy at the funeral and also spoke at the burial. Prior to his dad's passing, Bill had the same dream on three different occasions. In the dream, an old, trophy buck walked under his tree stand and looked up. It was as if this monarch of the forest was trying to tell him something. Bill raised his gun to shoot, but could not bring himself to pull the trigger. Bill tried to grasp the meaning of his dream, but understanding eluded him.

The morning of Frank's burial at Stonewall Jackson Cemetery in Lexington, Bill ascended up North Mountain to gather his thoughts for the graveside eulogy. As Bill traveled up the switchback trail, his mind's eye imagined his dad, clad in blue jeans and rainbow-colored suspenders, walking stick in hand, just beyond the next bend. "It would be great to see a deer this morning," he thought to himself. The sun rose above the valley below as he sat on the rock outcropping and finished writing the words for the eulogy. As he descended from the mountain he thought, "No deer today, I suppose."

Suddenly, and silently, there it was. Standing in the middle of the trail, a yearling buck, sporting his very first set of velvet-covered spike antlers. The young deer hopped off the trail. He started walking back up towards Bill, paced back and forth, and then walked up beside him. Bill thought the actions of the young buck were out of character for a wild whitetail. Within a few minutes the deer took two leaps down the mountain, turned to look back and then bounded off into the woods.

It was at this moment that Bill understood the dream which he had about the old buck prior to his dad's death. That buck was his father. The wise old patriarch. The one that had raised his son well, to be a survivor. The buck had lived a full and good life. He had gained love and respect from all who knew him. He was living out his final days. God would take him in His time. The young buck that morning was not a dream. Bill saw it as a living sign, sent by God. He said, "Through the buck, Dad was telling me that he had a brand new life, new places to go, new things to see. He wanted me to know that everything was all right and I didn't have to grieve his death."

With that assurance, Bill did not grieve his dad's death. Some years later he moved to a place he calls "The Pungo Prairie." His friend Willard Ashburn delivered an orphaned fawn to him. He has since received many others. Bill sees it as his dad asking the Lord to send him these little ones to nurture and have for a while. Bill concluded, "The Lord took me, a hunter, and taught me to be like a mother to the deer who no longer had one."

Before I left Bill's house, he gave me a DVD titled "My Little House on the Pungo Prairie," which shows him feeding baby deer goat's milk, teaching them to forage, and showing them love.

• • • • •

There was another reason I wanted to interview Bill. On Facebook I saw the response that he posted to his friend Velvet's status report: "Jesus, take the wheel." It was about an amazing experience he had some fifteen years prior, which I thought the reader would enjoy. So here it is:

"I will never forget that November night, 2:00 a.m. on a long stretch of road in Southern Manitoba, about 35 miles north of the U.S. border. Just me and my Bronco, set at 65 on cruise control. For the last 100 miles the highway had been clear of the black ice I had been driving on since leaving camp north of Big River at 4:00 the previous afternoon.

"Then all of a sudden, there it was. Up ahead, in the beam of my headlights, the pavement changed from dull gray to shiny black. A solid ridged line, transforming the safe road into a trail of terror. Black Ice! I hit the cruise button to coast. I knew that applying the brakes would surely bring disaster.

"I gripped the wheel tight to hold the truck steady as it hit the icy ridge. And then almost as if in slow motion even though I was still at nearly 60 mph, the truck and I were doing 360's as we slid towards the right shoulder and down the bank, hurtling towards the snow drift below. I cried aloud, 'Jesus! Jesus, take the wheel!' I really thought this could be 'it.'

"I felt like the truck was about to flip as it catapulted off of the ice towards the snow bank. Then in a blink, the Bronco settled sideways hard into what was also a cushion of powdery white. The force of the impact shut the engine off. And though shaken, I realized that the truck hadn't flipped. It was still on all fours resting in the snowdrift about 150 feet from the interstate. I was still alive!

"I turned the key in the ignition. The motor started. 'Thank You, Jesus!' I exclaimed. I said to myself, 'I think I can get out of here.' I reached into the glove box for my flashlight and went to the back of the truck to gather four sets of chains. I draped them, one by one, over each of the four tires. I turned the hubs, climbed back into the cab, selected '4X4 Low,' and rolled a quarter turn. I got back out to clip the chains secure. Sure enough, the chained tires gripped in and I drove the truck back to the steep shoulder of the road.

"Just then, an eighteen wheeler was approaching at a creep. The trucker got out of his rig and says, 'You okay?'... 'Thanks to the Lord I am!' I shouted back. 'I don't think I can pull you up the bank. It's too slick,' he replied as he was picking himself up from the fall he had just taken on the ice. 'It's okay,' I said. 'I have a winch on the front. If I can just hook a chain to that bar across the back of your trailer, I think I can winch her back to the top.' 'Okay,' he said. 'Let's try it!'

"Within thirty minutes my Bronco and I were creeping back along the icy road towards the United States of America. I sang hymns and praises aloud, all the way to the customs checkpoint. Jesus took the wheel! And He will take it for you, Velvet ... Of this I am certain. He will even send you a big rig and a trucker to haul your load back onto the road ... One day, they may even write a song about it."

ROY FLANAGAN, EXTENSION AGENT

Question: Is Pungo in the city or in a rural area?
Answer: Yes.

Unlike most major cities, Virginia Beach (the largest city in Virginia in population), has 25,000 acres of cropland, with 9,000 acres in an Agricultural Reserve Program which means that there most likely will never be less than 9,000 acres of farmland within the city limits. Pungo is strategically located between the rapidly growing urban development to the north of Indian River Road and the largely rural area that extends from Pungo to the North Carolina border.

The three largest contributors to the economy of Virginia Beach are the military, tourism, and agriculture. There are research farms known as Agricultural Research Centers scattered throughout the state, owned by Virginia Tech. The nearest one to Pungo is on Diamond Springs Road in Virginia Beach.

It was an educational experience for me to interview Roy Flanagan and to learn a great deal about his job as an extension agent for the City of Virginia Beach. Possibly some readers who are not farmers will not know much about this kind of work.

Roy and his wife Jeannie have five children: Colby, Bailey, Fletcher, Avonlea, and Lucas. Roy's job title is Agricultural and Natural Resources Agent (specializing in grains and commercial horticulture), a position he has held since February 2012. Some other extension agents in Virginia Beach are Horticulture (ornamental, landscape, etc.), Family Consumer Sciences (formerly known as Home Economics), and 4-H / Youth Development. All are part of the Virginia Cooperative

Extension Service, whose employees are based in every rural locality in the state of Virginia. Each is a local arm of Virginia Tech and Virginia State University. This year marks the 100th anniversary of the establishment of the Cooperative Extension Service by the Smith-Lever Act, signed into law by President Woodrow Wilson on May 15, 1914.

Actually, Roy has two jobs, as he is also a farmer himself. As well as raising strawberries, sweet potatoes, and other vegetables, he is in charge of the Flanagan turkey flocks, which includes turkey killings just before Thanksgiving and again shortly before Christmas – a major undertaking!

Roy is a graduate of Ferrum College, a small United Methodist college located near Rocky Mount, Virginia, with a degree in agriculture that he says prepared him well for his present work since it is a broad-based agriculture degree rather than one based on a narrow specialty. A good number of Ferrum graduates are currently working as extension agents in Virginia.

Since extension agents must have a Master's degree within six years of being hired, Roy is currently a student at Virginia Tech, with all classwork done via Internet. He expects to earn his degree by the end of 2016.

Asked about his duties as an extension agent, Roy said, "We do anything we can to help make farming profitable. We help sustain agriculture through scientific research and information." Often he is called about problems farmers are having. They might be about diseased plants, soil testing, nutrient issues, insects, and many other needs.

Roy also provides programs to educate farmers, bringing in specialists and researchers – an average of a dozen each year. The sessions are well attended, since many of them are linked to training classes for pesticide recertification. To be permitted to use pesticides, a license is required, and it must be kept current through recertification.

There are also regional meetings such as a crop conference and a Hampton Roads fruit and vegetable meeting. Once a year, in late February or early March, Virginia Beach and Chesapeake team up to provide a strawberry school that is attended by people from three states. The Virginia Beach extension service is probably best known for strawberries; they get questions about strawberries from all over the state.

Roy likes his job. "The job's pretty good," he says, "because I am working with good people." He is never truly off duty; he gets text messages, and he frequently sees farmers at church, at the 7-11, and other places in Pungo, but he says, "I'm fine with that. What I lack in book knowledge, I make up for by availability."

Roy's farm has been in the Flanagan family since 1913, but it has a history that dates all the way back to the Revolutionary War of the 1770's. His father, David Flanagan, was plowing the field directly behind the site where Roy has built his house, where a railroad track used to be, when his plow unearthed a cannonball. Roy was a small boy, and remembers seeing it. His mother, Susan Flanagan, took it to a museum in Hampton because she wanted to be sure it would not explode. She was told it was a Revolutionary War cannonball, but that it was harmless. It is now a family relic, located on a shelf in a cabinet in David and Susan Flanagan's family room. Roy says his father often found spear points and arrowheads, as well as the cannonball, probably because he did deep plowing, whereas nowadays most farmers are using disc plowing.

Final question: "What are the advantages of growing up on a farm?"

Answer: "What's not an advantage? – Appreciation for agriculture, knowing where food comes from, knowing what goes into producing it. I visit schools to help educate kids about agriculture, and one asked where I sleep – he thought I lived in a barn. Another advantage: the amount of freedom growing up on a farm – different from anywhere else. It's a privilege to grow up on a farm. Colby is just getting to drive the tractor by himself; the twins (Bailey and Fletcher) can only drive it out in the field."

As an agricultural extension agent, Roy is officially a member of the faculty at Virginia Tech, while at the same time, ironically, he is a Tech student. When asked whether that means he has the summer off, as many of the faculty members do, the expression on his face communicated "I can't believe anyone would ask that question." Even though Roy has much work to do all year round, summer is by far his busiest time!

JACK FENTRESS, GAME WARDEN / AIRPLANE PILOT

On September 4, 2013, I attended Fritzi Fentress' memorial service, and among the pictures shown was one of an airplane, reminding me that her husband Jack used to be an airplane pilot as well as game warden. A light bulb went on above my head with the thought, "It would be good to include a tale in Pungo Tales Four *about his experiences in that job."*

Jack began our interview by telling me that in the later years, when he was flying all over Virginia to work with other game wardens, he was often away from home and spent a lot of nights in motels. That meant that he missed church on many Sundays. However, a car was provided for him in each location where he landed, and if there was a church nearby he would drive to it. Even though it was interesting to travel, it was not like being at home.

His flying began in this area where the plane had not been used by previous game wardens. At first people were not accustomed to that kind of carrying on. A man would sit in the back of the boat so that the plane would not hit the boat.

There was a lot of duck hunting traffic in those days in Back Bay and surrounding waters. Johnnie Crumb often flew with Jack, and on one occasion they saw some men shooting ducks but not picking them up. They noticed that one of the men was Johnnie's uncle, and Jack asked Johnnie, "Do you want to go away and not give them a ticket?" Johnnie said, "No, even though he's my uncle, he's breaking the law and we have to stop him." Johnnie called him by name and said, "We have to give you a ticket!" The uncle cussed him, but Johnnie still wrote out his ticket. Later they took him to court. Jack said, "That's the way it should be done. If it's an aggravating case, you want to go to court to settle it once and for all."

In those days, duck traffic was plentiful whether the tide was high or low. Hunters could hide the ducks they had killed in traps and sell them in New York. Seldom did Jack catch the hunters at the traps because the hunters would come at night and take the ducks to send on to New York.

I asked Jack how he got into flying. He said, "When I got out of the service, with the help of the G.I. Bill, I went to flying school and got my pilot's license. Later I got the sea plane rating. In 1961 I started working for the state and worked for almost 30 years."

My next question was whether he had any accidents. He said, "Yes, I had two. The first one was early in the squirrel season. I flew out to Southampton County to check on the hunters. As a pilot I was familiar with that county. I got an early start that morning, after filling all three tanks with fuel. As I got over some pine trees, the motor started to sputter. Just ahead I saw a peanut field and headed toward it to put the plane down. As it hit the ground, I pulled the controls back toward myself. I called the state to report the accident. Then I talked with the land owner and told him that the state would reimburse him for the damage. His response was, 'No, I'm just glad you didn't get hurt!'

"The second one was right here on our property. I was trying to land on the path that leads to my neighbor's. I was with the new person who was to take my place when I retired. He was seated in the front seat and I was piloting from the back seat, which is always something difficult to do. One wheel got off the path enough to flip the plane over. Fortunately, neither one of us was hurt!"

Jack's co-worker Johnnie Crumb came to Jack and Fritzi's home as often as he could. He was always impressed with how clean Fritzi kept the house, especially the oven. The first thing he would do was to go to the kitchen and check the oven to see if it was clean. Then they would laugh at how well she had passed the uncertified inspection. Right after Fritzi died, Johnnie came to visit Jack, and again he checked the oven, which Fritzi had continued to keep clean even though she was not well.

The day before she died, Fritzi asked Jack how the grandkids and great-grandkids and some friends were doing. She especially asked about people in the church. For years she taught the women's Ruth Bible Class at church, and she went around in the car picking up people who didn't have transportation to church. She remembered her students and their families.

Jack enjoyed his work as a game warden very much and feels that it was a good experience and a challenge to work all over the state in addition to working locally. Obviously, he did a great job!

Back Bay, in the rural part of Virginia Beach near Pungo, where duck hunters were often observed by Game Warden Jack Fentress
(Photo by Walter A. Whitehurst)

KERMIT MITCHELL, WEDDING MAGISTRATE

In big cities it is not unusual to find wedding magistrates. A quick search on the internet will bring up such sites as "tietheknot.com." (Yes, that is an actual website.) However, who would expect to find a wedding magistrate in rural Pungo?

In recent years, every time I went along Mill Landing Road, I noticed a sign in front of Kermit Mitchell's house on the road that says "Wedding Magistrate," which made me want to talk with him about weddings he has performed. I had seen him on some occasions at Asbury United Methodist Church, but had not had an opportunity to ask him about it. So I set up an appointment to meet with him, and when I knocked on his door I saw a sign that said "Elder Kermit Mitchell." I am happy to include what I learned in that conversation.

Kermit is an ordained clergyman and therefore has been licensed to counsel with couples and to perform weddings. He is African American, and most of his weddings have been performed for white couples, although he has also provided the ceremony for some African Americans, possibly those who are not involved in church.

When he meets with a couple, he starts by making certain that they know what the Bible says about marriage. If they say they are willing to do that, he sets up another appointment with them. If they are not interested, he wants to know if they are willing to jeopardize God's word. He asks if either or both of them have been married before. If so, he wants to know what happened to the previous marriage. Again he stresses with them the value of having a deep faith in God, and he encourages them to worship God together in the same church.

Kermit went on to share something about his and Georgia's marriage 55 years ago. At that time he was not really a Christian and had not been saved. He did not treat his wife with respect and was not considerate of her feelings. He was very demanding that she beckon to his every wish. But 40 years ago he was saved, and his life changed.

When Kermit was ordained, he was invited by the Bishop in North Carolina to serve a pastorate there. After praying about it and considering it, he declined to go. It became clear to him that his pastoral work would be to preach in many churches where he was invited. That way he was free to preach God's Word with clarity without worrying about who might be offended. He has continued to live in his own house here in Virginia Beach.

When asked what his work was in the early years of his life, Kermit said that he worked on local farms during the week. He especially recalls walking behind a fast-moving mule to plow the fields. It was hard for him to keep up with the mule. Finally, he came up with the idea of making a small cart in which he could ride and there was no longer a problem of keeping up with the mule. Pulling the cart made the mule walk slower. Not everybody would have thought of that solution.

In his early elementary years he studied at the Pleasant Ridge School, a one-room building located on the property of Asbury United Methodist Church. In recent years, his secular work has been with landscaping.

When asked if there is some funny experience that happened during a wedding, he immediately told about a wedding in Creeds. When it was time to start the wedding, there was a dog right where Kermit was to stand. Dogs and Kermit are not good friends, and it became obvious to everyone that he was afraid of the dog. The groom saved the day for Kermit, as he quickly took the dog away and put it up away from the site of the wedding. For a brief moment, Kermit forgot what he was there for. It finally occurred to him that it was time to have a wedding. As we might say, "Dog Gone it!" The rest of the wedding went very well.

RITA JOYNER AND THE SILVER TAPPERS

I first got to know Rita when she and Velma Cartwright, along with some other persons, joined Betty and me on a cruise in November 2007 which was called "Paul's Fourth Missionary Journey." In addition to seeing the places along the way where St. Paul went to Rome as a prisoner and hearing lectures about what happened to Paul in each location, we went through a major storm that occurred while we were on the Ionian and Mediterranean seas on our way to Malta. We were reminded that on Paul's journey, even though he was a prisoner, he suggested they not go to Malta because of bad storms in the fall. They paid no attention to Paul and ended up with the sinking of their ship. We also paid no attention to Paul, for we too went through a bad storm with plates, glasses, and silverware falling off dining room tables and some people falling and suffering injuries.

The other place where I have gotten even better acquainted with Rita is at the exercise class she directs on Thursday mornings at the Senior Resource Center. The way she leads it, with musical accompaniment, it is obvious that she is an outstanding dancer. It occurred to me that others would like to read about her dancing career.

Rita was born in Virginia Beach, but she grew up in Norfolk. At three years of age, she started taking dance lessons. Each year she participated in the dance recital at the former Center Theater, now the Harrison Opera House. At seven or eight she even did solo dances, also at the Center Theater. She continued taking lessons for 29 years. She was involved in lots of dance shows at the Portsmouth Naval Hospital, where they performed for patients in the wards. She crossed over from Norfolk to Portsmouth in a boat that landed at the Naval dock. (There was no tunnel in those days.) There she did solos as well as performing with her class.

As a child, from four to twelve years old, Rita also danced and sang with the Joe Brown Radio Show which was broadcast live from Loews Theater, now known as the Roper Performing Arts Center of Tidewater Community College. I remember hearing the Joe Brown Radio Show myself and it may be that I heard Rita sing without knowing who she was.

Right after World War II, Rita performed at the USO in Portsmouth and at the Navy YMCA which was located in the former Union Mission building in Norfolk. She remembers the beautiful murals on the walls of that building, where there were dances for the families of the military servicemen. In Kecoughtan there was a nice auditorium at what is now the Veterans Administration Hospital, where they performed annually, soon after Christmas, traveling there by ferry.

Soon after graduating from Maury High School, Rita opened her own dance studio. With a smile on her face, she said, "I opened the business because I was too short to dance with the Rockettes!" She also started teaching dance for girls' clubs and the Recreation Center in Norfolk.

Eventually, her business moved from Norfolk to Virginia Beach. That business lasted for 46 years. I asked if it was time to retire after 46 years. She said, "Yes, the number of students started to decline due to growing interest in soccer and cheerleading. Also, it was getting to be time to slow down." Of course, it doesn't look like she slowed down very much. Not only does she lead a weekly exercise class; she also directs the Silver Tappers, a senior tap-dancing group which meets three times a week and performs twice a month. I have seen their presentations on several occasions, and they always do a great job. That group is always open to new persons who are interested in participating with them.

Finally, Rita said, "I am a third generation in Pungo because my grandparents were John Lovett and Lena Hartley, and I moved here to live on what was their property in the Pungo area."

Those of us who live in Pungo are fortunate to have Rita Joyner in our midst.

III.

PUNGO –

PAST AND PRESENT

TRIBES, A MOVIE MADE IN PUNGO

In 1995, at the age of 25, Virginia Beach native Glenn McClanan, Jr., was a graduate student at New York University. For his thesis he wrote and directed a short film, "Tribes." Cast members are Michael Connor, Laura Robbins, Jimonn Cole, Bob Burchette, and Leonard Parker.

McClanan, whose family's history in the area dates back to the 1600's, wanted to return to his home town to make his thesis film. The film was shot in rural areas of Virginia Beach, with key scenes shot in the historic Great Dismal Swamp.

It is a fictional story of two neighboring farm families – one white and one black.

The movie begins with a voice talking from the swamp: "My daddy used to tell me the swamp is a place I should never go. Folks say the coloreds used to always escape there before the Civil War and their ghosts are still there. Sometimes late at night you could hear the ghosts calling. As a boy I used to go there sometimes. I kept thinking my mother's spirit might have gone out there to the swamp and maybe I might hear her calling." Then a pair of bloody hands are shown, being washed in the swamp.

The title, TRIBES, appears on the screen, followed by shots of a wheat field, a lone tree, a barn, then the farmhouse. The words "Princess Anne County, 1919" appear at the bottom of the screen.

A young man, Johnny Webb, Jr., arrives home from selling potatoes. His father comes out of the house and asks him, "How much did you get at the market today?" When he says

"Five cents a pound," the disappointed dad says, "Guess I should have gone myself," introducing one of the movie's themes – the conflict between father and son.

At that point, two African American neighbors – Creed and his dad – appear on the scene. Creed has on an army uniform, with a shiny medal on his chest. His father says proudly, "Creed is just back from the war. His captain said he had done so fine he could come home early, and now he plans to go to college." Mr. Webb says, "Least we got ourselves one war hero around these parts," and Creed's dad responds, "It's a shame Johnny was not accepted by the Army." Creed says, "I heard that Mr. Webb asked the Army office not to take his son."

The next theme – the relationship of Creed and his former teacher, Sally Webb – is introduced when Creed's father says to Creed, "Aren't you going to greet your teacher?" Sally looks out the window and then comes to the door, where she and Creed greet one another. Mr. Webb says, "Baby Sal wanted to go to college, but she had too much to do around here, with her momma gone" – indicating there is another conflict within the family.

The third theme of the movie becomes evident when Creed's father says as he and Creed walk away, "Son, over in France they treated you all nice. It's different here – you're home."

The next day Sally puts on her finest clothes and leaves the house after telling her brother, "I'm going to the Kellers' but don't tell Daddy." Next we see Johnny whittling on the porch. Mr. Webb appears and says, "We're going to kill us a hog today." Johnny asks, "Can I do it?" Mr. Webb questions whether Johnny can stand it. Then he explains how to use the knife to cut the hog's throat, and the son puts the knife at the hog's throat but says, "I can't. The pig is too small." His dad says, "We need the money. That's part of being a farmer. That's part of being a man." With that, Johnny leaves and his dad kills the pig.

In the following scene Johnny is walking in the swamp and hears Sally calling for Creed, who comes to her and they kiss. As Johnny watches, Creed gives Sally a wrapped gift – his diary from the war. She says, "At least one of us is going to college." Creed replies, "I want you to go with me." She says, "My daddy would come after us!" Then she runs after Creed.

Later, at dusk, we see Mr. Webb and Johnny going out with lanterns. They go to Creed's house, knock on the door, and when Mr. Keller, Creed's dad, comes out, Mr. Webb says, "You seen Baby Sal and that son of yours?" He replies, "They're gone, Mr. Webb – he just rushed in and left – didn't say." After some threatening remarks from Mr. Webb, Creed's father tells him that they headed out toward Chesapeake.

The next morning, Creed and Sally are walking through the swamp. Elsewhere in the swamp, Johnny and his dad have been walking and stop for a break. Johnny asks, "Why do you think the Army office didn't accept me?" Precisely at that moment they hear a sound, and Mr. Webb picks up one of his guns and they go after Creed and Sally.

As she begins running, Sally's long dress gets caught in the underbrush, and she loses sight of Creed. Mr. Webb shoots in the direction of the noise. Creed comes up behind him, knocks him down and takes the gun and runs away. Mr. Webb catches Sally and slaps her, with Johnny watching.

The scene switches to a campfire at night. Johnny talks with his sister while their dad sleeps. He tells her, "Daddy's just concerned for the family's sake." She asks, "What about what I want?" He explains that he has to obey his dad because he wants to run the farm someday. She tries to convince him that their dad is bad – especially how much he mistreated their mother. Johnny goes to sleep, and in his dream he relives the moment when as a young boy he went into the barn and saw his mother hanging from a rafter.

The next morning, on the edge of the swamp, Johnny says, "Daddy, you do believe in me, don't you?" His dad replies, "Well, of course I do, Son," and concludes, "When someone tries to steal something away from you, you gotta stop 'em."

As they walk down the path, Sally's hands are tied to a rope around Johnny's waist. They find a boat and get in it and begin to catch up with Creed, who shoots the gun at them, and yells, "Let her go!" Mr. Webb takes his other gun and chases him.

In the next scene Creed and Sally are embracing, and Mr. Webb aims the gun at them. Mr. Webb says, "Move away, girl!" Creed pushes her aside as Mr. Webb aims the gun at him. Then he lowers the gun and asks Johnny to tie them up. Johnny ties Sally to one tree and Creed to another one, and tells his dad, "I'll go get the boat." Mr. Webb says, "Wait a minute, Son. You ain't finished yet. Get your knife out – just like on the farm." Johnny puts his knife to Creed's throat, then says, "I can't." His dad laughs at him and says, "I knew you didn't have it in you," and raises his gun to fire. Johnny says, "I can't let you do that."

Mr. Webb says, "Just try to stop me." When Johnny hesitates, Mr. Webb says, "Just like the day I went down to the Army office. You just ain't enough man for the Army. Not enough for running the farm." Again he aims his gun at Creed, and Johnny says, "Daddy, I can't let you." Mr. Webb says, "Well, stop me – come on, just stop me – you can do it (as he laughs) – you don't have it in you. . . . You just ain't man enough – not for the Army, not even for running a farm."

Johnny kills his father, slitting his throat with the knife, just the way his father had taught him to kill the pig. They bury the body and put up a cross of two branches. Sally and Creed leave. Johnny washes his bloody hands in the swamp (a repeat of the introductory scene) and then he is seen rowing the boat.

The last scene shows Johnny at home and ends with him saying, "Quiet is what I want now, more than anything else at all." Once again there are views of the farm, followed by the closing statement:

– Written, directed and produced by Glenn McClanan –
– For my mom and dad –

A TALE OF TWO PONIES
(As told by Joe Burroughs)

When he was a boy, Joe had two ponies. One was named Trixie, a girl, and the other one was Smokey, a boy. They were quite different, not only in gender. As we tell their stories you will see how different they were.

The first one was Trixie, a pretty gentle pony that was generally very calm. She was obedient and tried to do whatever Joe wanted her to do, to the best of her ability. Many of Joe's friends rode her often, and none of them was ever thrown off. One day Joe was riding her on Indian River Road toward the east when he noticed an empty house on the right-hand side of the road. The doors and windows were open, and so Joe decided to ride Trixie right through the open door. Inside, they went from room to room and got to know the house very well. Weldon Land happened to see them roaming through the house. He stopped them and said to Joe, "I saw what you were doing, and I'm going to tell your dad," which of course he did. Joe's dad, Fred, went to make sure there was no damage done to the house. (He even found it amusing, but he made it clear that Joe should not do that again.)

Another thing Trixie liked to do was to climb up the steps of the porch around the store in Pungo Village which at that time was called G. W. Land & Son (more recently John Munden's Store). However, like a cat that can climb up a tree but cannot climb down the tree, she was afraid to even try to climb down the store's steps. Therefore, it was necessary for Joe to ride her around the store to a back porch that did not have any steps. People enjoyed gathering around and watching Trixie go up the steps with Joe on her back. One person would buy a Coca-Cola and watch her drink it down with much gusto as the bottle was held up for her. One reason she liked to walk on the store porch was that when she arrived from Norfolk, she was unloaded on the porch around the store across the road which belonged to the Burroughs family. Joe's dad had purchased her and he asked Louis Walters, who constantly took produce from his fields to sell at the Norfolk farmers' market, to bring her to Pungo.

The second pony was Smokey, a horse of a different color, figuratively speaking. His dad Fred asked Joe to break Smokey in, but his attempts were not successful. So Fred asked Roy Caffie to do it. The two boys mounted Smokey with Roy in front and Joe behind, wrapping his arms around Roy's waist. Smokey threw them both off quickly, with Joe landing on top of Roy. Then Roy asked Joe if he wanted to ride in the front, and Joe's response was "Absolutely not!" Roy said that his uncle Cecil could do it. They hitched Smokey to a cart, and Cecil with his strong arms was able to control Smokey until one rein broke and Smokey ran wild. Cecil jumped out of the cart, just in time.

One day Joe's mother Malvine and their neighbor Patti Bonney asked Joe to take trash to dump in the woods beside Indian River Road. He hitched Smokey to the cart and put trash cans in it. Kermit Land, Jr., Horace Van Nostrand, and Snooky Mosley went with Joe in the cart. Off they went with no problem and dumped the trash. After they started back home, the empty cans started to rattle, which scared Smokey, and he began to run out of control. Kermit jumped out of the cart with no problem, but Horace also jumped out and landed on the hard-surfaced part of the road and hit his chin. They had to take him to the hospital. Joe lost control of Smokey, and finally the cart turned over. Kermit thought that Joe was killed, and he ran and told Joe's parents that the cart turned over and Joe was dead. Fortunately, Joe was all right.

Many persons tried to ride Smokey, but he threw most of them off. Dick Luxford tried to ride him, but before he fell off, he shouted, "Help! Help! Help!" Dick never came back again. Joe said that he never did completely break Smokey.

One time I tried to ride him, and he threw me off. Joe remembers that I shouted, "My leg is broken," but I quickly remembered that whenever Smokey threw someone off, he immediately ran and tried to take a bite. All of a sudden, my leg was miraculously healed and I got up and ran away!

"WHATEVER HAPPENED TO . . . ?"
(As told by Joe Burroughs)

Many of the buildings that used to be in Pungo Village are now gone. Some have disappeared completely, others have been moved to new locations, and some are still standing but are used for a different purpose. Below are descriptions of some of the changes in recent years.

Our imaginary journey through long-ago Pungo begins on the west side of Princess Anne Road, just north of Indian River Road.

Dr. Snead's Office

At one time there were two doctors in Pungo: Dr. Luxford, whose house and office were immediately south of the present Pungo Square shopping center, and Dr. Snead. Dr. Snead's office building, which no longer exists, was located in the front yard of the Ellis Dixon house which is still standing and is the first house on the left side of Princess Anne Road just beyond the traffic light going north.

Dr. Snead was Mrs. Dixon's father. He practiced medicine as well as doing a small amount of farming. One day Dr. Snead told a friend that someone was stealing some of his chickens, and he suspected that it was the African American man who worked for him on the farm. That night Dr. Snead and his friend went to check that man's chickens. They got out of there as quickly as they could when the bulldogs barked at them and caused a ruckus among the chickens. The next day the black man said, "Dr. Snead, the same men that steal your chickens tried to steal mine last night, but the dogs scared them away!"

After Dr. Snead closed his office, the building was used as a restaurant run by Mr. Saddlethite, who was famous for his oyster meals. It later became a private home until it was torn down.

Dr. Snead's office (left) and the Dixon house (right)
(Photo provided by Joe Burroughs)

Pallett's Palace and Henley's Stand

Henley's Stand, selling fruits and vegetables, until recently stood on the northwest corner of Princess Anne Road and Indian River Road, where Pallett's Palace was previously located. Pallett's had a state permit to sell alcohol. Before it was Pallett's, it belonged to Roy Whitehurst, who hired Earl Munden to run the store. One day in the wintertime, Earl had kerosene in a can that had been used for gasoline, and when he threw kerosene on the wood stove, it flamed up and burned Earl's body badly. A customer was able to put out the fire, so no other damage was done, but Earl was taken to the hospital and later died.

In the 1920's there was a small mechanic shop on the north side of Pallett's Store, attached to the building. It held three or four cars, and the mechanic was Noe Garrett. South of Pallett's was the Whitehurst barbershop, described in "The Moving of a Barbershop ... and More," on page 77 of this book.

Turning west on Indian River Road, we pass a few houses before coming to the Pungo Ice Plant on the left.

The Pungo Ice Plant

The ice plant was located on Indian River Road west of the traffic light. Before people had electricity, they put ice from the ice plant in the non-electric ice boxes in their homes. It was a cotton gin in earlier days when local farmers raised cotton. When the area switched from cotton to potatoes, there was also a barrel factory in that same location. When the potato grading started at the train station, they began to pack potatoes in the barrels but had to stop it because the barrels bruised the potatoes. So the farmers went back to putting the potatoes in burlap bags.

Returning to Princess Anne Road, we again head south on the west side of the road.

Dozier and Eaton's Store

Joe Burroughs' dad owned the store building located on the southwest corner of Princess Anne Road and Indian River Road. One of the early occupants of the building was Dozier and Eaton's Store. When Joe's dad purchased that property, the store had been closed for several years. When it was demolished, someone asked Joe why he was tearing it down, and he said, "We had to because the termites were holding hands to keep it together."

Aaron Carroll's Mechanic Shop

Continuing south on Princess Anne Road, there were two buildings that were built by Aaron Carroll – a mechanic shop and a service station. Mr. Carroll ran the mechanic shop, and Thuggett Bonney opened an ESSO (Standard Oil) station in the other building. Derwood Bonney started that business and his son Elroy ran it, and Thuggett later bought the business.

Thuggett Bonney's Station

In addition to selling gas, Thuggett Bonney sold tires and oil, washed cars and Simonized (polished) them, but he did not do mechanical work. He had a lot of business, especially in the summer, due primarily to the fact that many trucks that came to haul potatoes bought tires there.

Styron's Barber Shop and John Os Capps' Apartment

Beside Thuggett Bonney's station there was a building which had Ernest Styron's barbershop in the front and an apartment at the side and back where John Os Capps lived for many years.

The Pungo Train Station

A short distance south there was a railroad track, which was built in southern Princess Anne County in 1889, and the Pungo Train Station. In the earlier days many passengers rode on the train to Norfolk, but with better roads and more vehicles, the train was used mostly for cargo. Since potatoes were the big crop in those days, trucks came from many parts loaded with locally grown potatoes and delivered to the train station where they were graded and sent on to Norfolk and up north. You could see long lines of trucks on Princess Anne

Road and Indian River Road. One hundred boxcars were loaded in 24 hours, each with 300 one-hundred-pound bags, totaling 30,000 bags a day.

The crew leaders were paid, and they in turn paid their workers, often taking advantage of the workers. The farmers made good money, but the crew leaders made more. They rode around in expensive cars and wearing fancy clothes. One crew leader had a '47 Chrysler Town and Country with triple horns on the front that played all kinds of tunes. Some crew leaders would fly to New York for the weekend.

Allan Brock's first job was to work Saturdays at the potato grader at the Back Bay Station. One Saturday he was asked to fill in at the Pungo station, and for a while he worked two shifts, one at Back Bay and one at Pungo.

One day one of the young boys in Pungo suggested to his friends, "Let's buy some soft drinks for five cents and sell them for ten cents at the potato grader, and then we'll take the bottles back and get the refunds." They had a good business going until the Superintendent said they might get hurt and made them stop their business.

Now we move across the road to the east side of Princess Anne Road, going north.

Princess Anne Telephone Company

Heading north on the right-hand side of Princess Anne Road, the first house is that of George W. and Lizzie Land, where the Princess Anne Telephone Company switchboard was located. Most people were on party lines, and the operators listened in on conversations. Being in charge of the switchboard almost worked Miss Lizzie to death. She had to stay there if one of the operators was sick. She even rented an upstairs bedroom at the Burroughs home across the road, so she could get away from the pressure of the switchboard.

Pop Carmine's Barber Shop and Guy Capps' Office

The front section of the next building on the right was a barbershop run by Pop Carmine. (Yes, Pungo had three barbershops at that time.) In the back Guy Capps had his office, from where he ran the potato business. The building was later moved to Indian River Road East, where it became a part of the Pungo Fish House.

Land & Capps Store

North of the barbershop is the store that was Land & Capps and more recently John Munden's store. It is still standing, although it is unoccupied at present. Originally George W. Land had a store on Princess Anne Road north of Pungo Village across from what is now Sherwood Lakes. That store opened in the early 1800's and was closed during the 1920's when he built a new store in Pungo and changed its name from Land & Capps to G.W. Land & Son.

Fentress' Store

On the northeastern corner of Princess Anne Road and Indian River Road were two buildings built by Clay James, who had the reputation of being an adventurous risk-taker. Apparently he was successful with his adventures. The first one was Fentress' Store, where men often gathered at night to play dominoes.

Moore's Mechanic Shop

The next building built by Clay James was Moore's mechanic shop. One thing that stood out is that on the north side of the roof someone had painted in big letters a sign:

P U N G O

That was done long before the Pungo Naval Airfield was built during World War II just north of the shop. The pilots landing at the airfield during the war enjoyed seeing that sign! *(The Pungo Naval Airfield was described in the original* Pungo Tales.*)*

When all of the above buildings were standing, primarily during World War II and afterwards, Pungo was full of people on Friday and Saturday afternoons and evenings. Farmers came to do their shopping, get haircuts, and visit with friends. Stores stayed open until 11:00 those nights, and things were hopping during that time. A survey of Pungo in 1950 reported that Pungo (some called it Downtown Pungo, and now some call it Pungo Village) was ¼ square mile and had a population of 175.

There are fewer houses today than in those days, and also fewer people live here. It seems that there are some possible reasons for that: Potatoes are no longer being raised in this area, and the railroad is no longer here. The Pungo Naval Airfield is no longer here. Nearby supermarkets made it impossible to keep the country stores open. Nevertheless, Pungo is still a vibrant community that plays a significant role within the City of Virginia Beach.

THE PUNGO RIDGE WINERY

Fred Havens moved to Pungo in 1987, where he lives with his dad Gene Havens. Fred studied at Tidewater Community College and later at the Art Institute in Atlanta. He worked at the Newport News Shipyard as a nuclear pipefitter at night and used the day to take photos. After a while he started getting more jobs taking pictures and eventually he went full time. For ten years he even had a studio on 21st street in Norfolk. The economy declined after 9/11, and it was difficult to make a living with photography, so he moved his business to Pungo where he converted a two-car garage into a studio.

One day his sister gave him six blackberry plants as a gift. After a year, he made some bottles of blackberry wine. The following year he produced more wine, and he started giving a bottle to couples when he did the photography work for their weddings. A year later he again made wine and did a lot of reading about how to produce wine. Johnnie Steele made wine, and he gave some of his recipes to Fred. That resulted in some of the first authentic wine.

When Fred's neighbor, Evelyn Gray, tasted the wine he made from strawberries, she said to him, "That is the best strawberry wine I have ever tasted. Don't change a thing!" That encouraged him to keep on making wine. Strawberries are very important in Pungo, so that was a wise choice.

With continuing support and encouragement, Fred began to think about opening his own establishment. His dad Gene helped by filling out the paperwork for securing an ABC license. Gene is the administrative manager; Fred makes the wine and is the producer, which means he decides what to do.

Fred's dad, Gene Havens, was the photo director for the Naval Audiovisual Center in Virginia Beach, covering all of Hampton Roads, prior to his retirement.

The first year Fred was blending and the second he was using pears and blueberry and fermented honey wine from honey bees with strawberries and blueberries purchased from local farmers. Next year he will make wine from eight fruits. Fred's business is small, and he plans to keep it that way. He has three hives of honey bees which produce forty pounds of honey per hive. His is the first and only winery in Virginia Beach. He gets free publicity because his business is listed in the Virginia Winery Guide 2013. This means that during the summer he has a lot of business because groups traveling on wine-tasting tours come to his business. So this new Pungo business brings a lot of tourism to Pungo and Virginia Beach, and many times the tourists stay in hotels and eat in local restaurants.

Fred says that he got into the winery business through the back door. Sharing his homemade wine with his customers in his photography work led him in this direction. And of course, he still continues to work as a photographer.

Can you picture that?

THE "CREATURE" AT CHARITY PRESHOOL
(As told by June Kernutt)

Shortly after I retired and returned to Pungo, I was invited to be the Associate Pastor of my childhood church, Charity United Methodist Church. One of my duties was to visit families whose children attended Vacation Bible School and the preschool. While visiting these families, I often heard the statement, "Charity Church really loves children!" That statement was especially made about the preschool program, one of the outstanding ministries of the church.

Charity Preschool was started in September 1985. It was the dream of Joan Atkinson (the wife of Steve Atkinson), who established the preschool, set everything in place, and was a wonderful director. June said, "The success of the preschool is due to her." The preschool began with a three-year-old-class and a four-year-old-class.

June's son Marty was in the preschool in its first year, and she was later the preschool director. Now her granddaughter is in the preschool, so theirs is a three-generation preschool family, and June has been a preschool parent, director, and now grandparent. When June was preschool director, her husband Martin was a partner in her work. At that time the church did not have adequate janitorial service, so Martin willingly came in to change light bulbs, install door knobs, and do whatever other tasks needed to be done.

Bill Mahon was the pastor when the preschool began. He would greet the parents every morning, calling each one by name. He was much loved by the parents and by the children. During that first year there was a Thanksgiving feast, and the children dressed as Pilgrims and Indians. Pastor Bill sat with the children in a circle on the floor – a very big man with a group of very small children.

When Bob Cooper was Charity's pastor, he was very involved with the preschool. The first time he went to lead the chapel service, June asked the children, "Do you know who this is?" Jeb Cullipher said, "Creature Bob!" From that time on he was known as Creature Bob by all the children, rather than as Preacher Bob. The preschool later gave Bob a name plate that said "Creature Bob" which he kept on his desk as long as he was at Charity Church.

Charity Church has always been supportive of the preschool. Church members, even those who do not have children in the preschool, step in when they hear of a need. The preschool has a policy that no child is turned away because the family cannot afford to pay. This is done on faith, and church members have always found a way to provide the necessary funds. One church member, hearing of a family whose father lost his job, took $50.00 to Ansell's grocery store and told them to let that family use the money for groceries. June told the mother to go there and get food for her family. More recently, an anonymous donor paid for one month's tuition for a five-year-old whose family was having financial problems.

The church supports the preschool by providing facilities for the office, classrooms, playground, and other activities as well as financial assistance. The preschool also contributes to the church by making improvements to the classrooms and bathrooms and attracting people to participate in church activities.

The teachers do more than just teach – they clean the classrooms and bathrooms every day. "The best part," says June, "is that everyone is there for the same reason, and they work together as a team. No one is too good to do a lowly job, and no one is too lowly to do whatever is needed. One may clean a bathroom if necessary, and if that person can't do it, another one will pitch in and do it. Teachers serve as mentors for teacher assistants so that someday they can be teachers."

Susan Flanagan has been a preschool teacher for many years, teaching the three-year-old class. At the end of the 2013-14 year she will have taught all seven of her grandchildren: Allie and Emmie Irving, and Colby, Fletcher, Bailey, Avonlea, and Lucas Flanagan.

Some children come for five days, some for three, and some for two. In 2011, the preschool began offering aftercare when morning classes are over, so that children whose parents both work can stay for the afternoon, with organized play and different kinds of learning projects.

Most preschool parents are not church members, but many have become members, thanks to the preschool. Whether they join the church or not, preschool parents are considered a part of the Charity Church family. One day a parent who attends another church asked if he could go into the sanctuary to pray, and of course his request was honored.

The preschool is a wonderful ministry. The teachers could work somewhere else for a lot more money, but they feel called to be in a church preschool, and they go far beyond just teaching. Once a child left a stuffed animal – the one he always slept with – in his classroom, and when he got home the mother called the preschool in a panic over the toy. The teacher told her not to worry about it, and took it by their house on her way home.

The preschool is grateful that church members have taken

care of the water testing requirement (since the church does not have city water). At first the director could take water samples and the state sent someone to test the water every three years. Later, when June Kernutt was the director, the state required that the water also be tested for E-coli monthly by a licensed Class 6 Waterworks Administrator, and there would be no help from the state. To get that license required a huge amount of reading, passing a test and then keeping the certification up to date. Johnnie Steele, a member of Charity's Board of Trustees, volunteered to do that. After Johnnie died of lung cancer, Steve Baggs, another church member, stepped up. By then the requirements had grown to include 2,000 hours of training. Steve is currently being trained, with an interim person being paid to sample the water once a month.

Heather Harris, the current director, was hired by the Board of Directors while she was still living in California. Since her husband was being transferred to the Virginia Beach area, she found the announcement for that position and submitted a resume that was so good that the committee interviewed her by phone. They told her it was basically a full-time job at a part-time salary. When she and her husband calculated what she needed to help pay the bills, it was that exact amount. June said, "It was a God thing!"

Here is a list of the preschool directors: Joan Atkinson (1985-1999); Ruth Massey (1999-2000); June Kernutt (2000-2003); Jennifer Bernhard (2003-2004); Yolanda Carila (2004-2006); Nancye Flinn (2006-2009); and Heather Harris (2009-present).

What is the preschool like for the children? June remembers that she would often ask the children, "How are you doing today?" One of them, Hunter Henley, would always reply, "G-r-r-r-r-eat!"

PUNGO GOES GLOBAL

One night at the Wednesday supper at Charity United Methodist Church, as we were waiting in line to get our meal, I met a new person, Lisa von Schlichting. When we started talking, I enjoyed her delightful accent. I immediately asked where she was from, and she said South Africa. I invited her to eat at our table. Naturally, I told her about my Pungo Tales *books and asked if she and her husband Eddi would be willing for me to include their story in* Pungo Tales Four. *She said "Yes!" Here is what I learned about them:*

Eddi has a degree qualifying him to be a dental technician, which means he makes false teeth, dental implants and bridges, etc. After working several years in laboratories in South Africa, he learned that there were openings for qualified technicians in America. A friend in America called to tell him about an opening. He was interviewed by phone and took the job by phone. He was immediately offered a position in Charleston, West Virginia.

Dental technician was one of the few occupations needed at that time in the USA. Since technicians in our country study only two years and in South Africa four years is required, Eddi was considered highly skilled and was therefore welcomed as an immigrant, along with his entire family.

They had no knowledge of Charleston, but Eddi thought, "It can't be a bad place; after all, it's the capital of a state in America." Lisa added, "And they've written a song about it, 'Almost Heaven, West Virginia.' " It was a leap of faith. Eddi and Lisa literally got down on their knees and said, "Lord, we're going to give this to you!" From all appearances, they have been richly blessed.

The people at Eddi's new place of work made all the arrangements for the family's visas and travel. They arrived in Charleston in 2002 after flying 27 hours to a small airport on top of a large mountain, in the dark, with their eight-year-old daughter Chanel and their five-year-old twins Jenna and Martin. They had sold all their belongings and got on the plane with ten big duffel bags, as they were allowed only two pieces of luggage per person. They flew from South Africa to Europe, had one layover, then to Detroit, where they had another layover, and then got on their connecting flight to Charleston: a twelve-passenger prop plane, with all their luggage piled on the back seats.

Their apartment was on the 18th floor. A woman who lived in a nearby apartment knocked on their door and gave them a basket full of stuffed toys. She and her husband immediately became their adopted grandparents. Being used to having to take precautions in South Africa, they kept their door locked, with the safety latch on, at all times. She told them, "You really don't have to keep the latch on all the time." Soon they were leaving the door unlocked and the children were running back and forth from their apartment to the adopted grandparents' apartment. That couple still visits the von Schlichting family once a year, and the von Schlichtings go to visit them twice a year. The husband is now 85, and when they celebrated their 50th anniversary recently at the Homestead, Eddi and Lisa were included as their children, along with the couple's two daughters.

The family moved to Virginia in 2003 for a better job opportunity. In 2009, Eddi decided to start his own business, and they moved to Virginia Beach and opened their own dental laboratory in the garage of their house in the King's Grant area. It was another leap of faith. It began with only two employees, but now, in its fifth year, the lab has grown from two persons to fourteen, and is located in a building near Lynnhaven Mall. Eddi is the Removable technician and Lisa takes care of the office work. There are two additional partners and ten employees. Each morning at the lab begins with a prayer meeting, and even though it is not mandatory, everyone comes.

All his life Eddi has wanted to be a farmer. Therefore he recently bought property in the Creeds area, and they moved into their new home in August 2013. Lisa had a vegetable garden in Kings Grant and is excited about having a vegetable and herb garden in Pungo. Eddi wants to have real crops and raise chickens, pigs, and possibly other farm animals. He has already plowed the field and put down stakes for a chicken coop. Roy Flanagan, the extension agent for Virginia Beach (whose story is also in this book), is helping him begin his farming career.

Eddi's parents spend six months each year in Virginia. His dad wanted to buy an RV, and Eddi has already found one for him. It is now on their property, with a deck built onto it, for his parents to stay in when they come from South Africa. The twins, Jenna and Martin, like to ride dirt bikes, so they have prepared a bike trail around the edge of their property. Martin also likes skeet shooting, and there is plenty of room for him to do that. They attend Kellam High School and seem very content to be citizens of Pungo. Their older sister, Chanel, is a student at Virginia Tech in Blacksburg, Virginia.

When asked how things are different here from South Africa, Lisa said, "The American grocery stores are much larger." The first time she went into Walmart, she was overwhelmed with aisles of cereal which seemed to go on forever. The foods are different, and packaging is very different.

Measurements are not the same because the metric system is used in South Africa. They are very happy in America and feel they have been well received. Lisa said that they helped start a local Methodist Church in South Africa, and now she and her family are very happy to be in Charity United Methodist Church.

Welcome, von Schlichtings, to

"Pungo -- Crossroads of the World!"

IV.

SOME SPECIAL

PUNGO EVENTS

THE MOVING OF THE BARBER SHOP ... AND MORE
(As told by Kitty Bosher)

When I was a boy, I used to go to a barber shop run by Luther Whitehurst in Pungo Village. The barber shop was located across the road from Brock's Store and south of Pallett's (a combination bar and general store).

Three things that I remember about that barber shop are that it cost 25 cents for a haircut; that I heard a lot of gossip and cussing among the customers as they waited for their turn; and that often when I got into the barber's chair, Luther would say, "I've got to do a good job with this one!"

I never heard him say that when he cut anyone else's hair. Was it because I was a Whitehurst, or did he think I was ugly and therefore needed all the help I could get? I wish I had asked him that question before he died. That building is no longer where it used to be, and I was happy to find out that it had been relocated to Kitty Bosher's house – the old Oscar Chaplain house.

Kitty moved to Pungo in 1972 when she bought the house from O. S. Chaplain, whose son Stuart Chaplain had been raised there. Formerly a teacher, she ran the Pungo General Store after Brock's Store closed, renting the store building from Joe Burroughs. In her kitchen is a sign that Allan Brock had attached to the chimney and left in the store when it closed. The sign, which was framed by Kitty's mother, says:

**SMOKERS AND CHEWERS
will please spit on each other,
and not on the stove!**

Kitty plans to give that sign to Allan Brock, Jr. to hang on his own chimney somewhere down the road.

Larry Herz, Kitty's former husband, was very good at building and fixing things (which was really helpful when Pungo General Store came into being in 1980). The store had an amazing variety of things for sale, including home-baked bread, handmade wooden toys, and a rack of overalls, to mention a few. They also had Pungo T-shirts with a picture of the traffic light, reminiscent of the song, "Meet Me at the Stoplight Down in Pungo." Kitty used to say she bet she had the only store in the world that had tofu and scrapple in the same cooler! And the walk-in refrigerator had been moved over from Pallett's when that store was torn down.

The barber shop was across the road from Pungo General Store and south of "Pallett's Palace." After Pallett's was razed, Larry heard that the barber shop was available to be purchased, but that it had to be moved as soon as possible, or it would also be razed.

When I talked with Larry Herz, I learned that he bought it for $200. It took two hours to load, move, and unload the building, which cost another $200. Larry says, "For a total of $400, I believe it was one of the best deals I've ever made!"

The barber shop was moved at 8:00 on a Sunday morning, and since it was going only a short distance down the road, he decided not to get a permit. Sure enough, there was no traffic at all that morning... except for a police car. As they entered the driveway, the policeman appeared on the scene and asked to see the permit. Fortunately, the truck driver knew the policeman and talked him out of giving Larry a ticket.

After the move, the barber shop was located behind the house at the only place where the truck could successfully back in and make the arc in order to offload the building. Larry remembers the barber shop as a very nice building, 12' x 20' with a front porch and a tin roof. It was put on cinderblocks, and the 8' x10' cypress beam underneath which was no longer needed was given to John Paxson. He used it to make duck decoys, and was very grateful to have it.

The barber shop stood tall and proud for more than thirty years in its new location, and was a nice addition to the property. It was mostly used for storage, but also served as an extra bedroom for their family of six children, and for two years was actually used as a one-room schoolhouse where Kitty home-schooled her two youngest children.

If you are thinking that you would like to go and see the old barbershop, we have some sad news for you. On Wednesday, March 24, 2010, while Kitty was in California, a fire started in a pile of mulch at the base of a large willow oak tree in the back yard. The fire charred the siding on the back of the house, burned up two vehicles, outbuildings including the barbershop, a milk house from Steve Barnes' home place on McClanan Lane, and the two remaining willow oak trees of the six that were there when Kitty moved in. Fortunately, there was a strong west wind that day; otherwise the house would have burned down instead of the outbuildings.

Sitting around Kitty's kitchen table after we covered the story of the barber shop, Kitty told a story she had heard from her father, Pete Bosher, which she said "might even be true." He was at a Kentucky Fried Chicken one day and saw an old man outside picking up some trash. It was actually Colonel Sanders himself! And the lesson he drew from that experience was, "You can always tell who the owner is. It's the person who picks up the trash."

Kitty learned that lesson well, and along the way she even signed up with the City as "Friends of Flanagan Lane" (*now called Cayman Lane*) even though it was "Friend," not "Friends." Regardless, she would carry a trash bag with her on her daily walks and collect the various beer cans and such that folks tossed out of their car windows as they drove by. When someone asked her once why she picked up after other people, she said, "I'm not doing it for them, I'm doing it for the planet." A self-described "recycle-maniac," she also feels like there is no such place as "away" as in "Throw it away." We share a finite world. We need to take care of it and protect its resources.

Another story that came out of our kitchen table conversation is one she absolutely knows to be true, because she was there. Sitting around that very same table one afternoon with her sons Patrick and Michael, one of them expressed a concern about how he was going to earn the money to support a family when he was grown.

"Well, boys," she said, "I'm going to tell you some things I didn't know when I was your age," after which she had their undivided attention. "First of all," she said, "thirty is young. You don't really have to know what you're going to do when you are fifteen. You've got time.

"Secondly, if you work at a job that pays you a lot of money, you are going to spend a lot of money. If you work at a job that pays you less money, you will spend less money. But what people don't tell you, but what is absolutely true, is that what you are REALLY spending is your life. So… Whatever you do, make sure it is meaningful to you.

"And thirdly, since you can work any place on the planet, go looking for a job in an area you know you will be happy to be in when you are NOT at work. If you like cities, go live in a city. If you like warm weather, look for a job in the South... stuff like that."

Perhaps because of that conversation, Kitty's children are in far-flung places. Patrick Dooley, her oldest son, lives with his wife and three daughters in Berkeley, California. Michael Dooley, her second son, lives with his wife and two daughters in El Zonte, El Salvador. Sarah Herz, her daughter, lives in Yogyakarta, Indonesia, and Andrew Herz, her youngest son, lives in Charlottesville, Virginia.

Kitty also told her children, "Life is for learning, and the good news is... You're alive!"

Now that sounds just like a person who would move an abandoned barber shop from one site in Pungo to her own back yard!

THE LOST PICTURES
(As told by Jeffrey R. Bek)

Dr. Bek is my dentist here in Pungo. He purchased some copies of my three Pungo Tales *books and put them on display with magazines so that patients could see them as they waited to see the doctor. Some of them asked where they could buy them. Kimberly, the receptionist, called and asked me to bring copies over to the office, resulting in several sales. When I asked Dr. Bek if he had a tale to share with me to be published in* Pungo Tales Four, *he told me the following interesting story.*

Dr. Bek was born in Iowa and lived there in his early days. While he was still a child, his parents got a divorce. He and his brother stayed with his mother and there were several moves from place to place. Eventually she married again, but that marriage also ended in divorce. During his high school days, they lived in Roanoke, Virginia, and he graduated from high school there.

In the course of their many moves, they lost a box containing pictures of his early life, to the sorrow of his mother. Whenever a family has a fire in which they have lost all their personal belongings, often they will grieve over not having pictures of earlier days.

In Buchanan, Virginia, there lives an elderly couple who loves to go to yard sales. Whenever they come across something like pictures, for example, they make an effort to locate the people to whom those pictures belong. That's exactly what they did when they found the box of pictures of the Bek family.

When they were trying to locate the family they were

able to get in touch with Dr. Bek's grandmother on his father's side in Iowa, and were then directed to Dr. Bek. It took a lot of research, but when they finally found Dr. Bek's address they sent the pictures to him immediately at their own expense. Dr. Bek was able to return the lost pictures to his mother on Mother's Day! His mother was very happy when Dr. Bek took the pictures to her after they had been lost for so many years.

There are still a lot of nice people in this world.

The office of Dr. Jeffrey R. Bek in Pungo Village
(Photo by Walter A. Whitehurst)

A VERY SPECIAL WEDDING

On September 21, 2013, I had the privilege and honor of officiating for the wedding of Glenn B. McClanan, Jr. and Julia Chen at the Berkeley Plantation in Charles City, Virginia. They invited me to do that because I had officiated at the funeral of Glenn's father, Glenn B. McClanan, Sr.

At the beginning of the ceremony I explained that Glenn Sr. and I grew up together. His parents and my parents were good friends, and Glenn and I were good friends. As children we often played together and as youth we double dated together. One summer we worked together as surveyor's helpers when the U.S. Navy built the jet runways at Fentress Airfield which provided space for Naval jets from Oceana Naval Airfield to practice landing and taking off to prepare for landing and taking off on carriers.

When Betty and I were married, her parents were not able to come from Texas for the wedding, and Glenn Sr.'s father, Herman McClanan ("Mr. Mac"), walked Betty down the aisle in place of her dad. I was very happy when Glenn Sr. and Reba were married because they were just right for each other.

There were about ninety people present for the wedding in the beautiful Berkeley Plantation Rose Garden, with the James River in the background. The weather forecast had called for rain about the time of the wedding. There was a nearby tent for the reception banquet following the ceremony, and plans were made to move to the tent in the event of rain.

Before the ceremony started we began to feel sprinkles, and people had umbrellas open over their heads. The musical trio moved to the tent to protect their instruments from getting wet. Just before starting, I asked Glenn if he wanted to move to the tent. He said, "No, I want us to go ahead with it in the open air."

I went to my position and the others came in as planned. Before starting, I showed the congregation my umbrella and said, "My experience is that when I have an umbrella in my hand it usually doesn't rain." Sure enough, the rain did not get too heavy, and it was a beautiful service. One very special part was a beautiful solo sung by Katie McClanan, daughter of Glenn's brother Martin.

While pictures were taken of the bride and groom and their attendants, hors d'oeuvres and drinks were being served in the tent. Then an elegant banquet was served, followed by dancing and toasts. Glenn and Julia live in New York City. Forty years ago, Julia's family moved from Taiwan to Brazil. I enjoyed speaking Spanish with her father, Mario Chen, who of course speaks Portuguese as well as Taiwanese and Mandarin Chinese.

Many of Julia's family members and friends came from Brazil for this special event. Because she is from Brazil, the dinner served after the rehearsal the night before the wedding included barbecue from Brazil and Virginia. There was a little competition between the two barbecues although there was never a vote on which of them won.

As you have read this story of the wedding, I hope you could feel some of the joy and excitement that a little bit of rain could not dampen.

(See Photo on Next Page)

Rev. Walter A. Whitehurst with the bride and groom
(Photo provided by Glenn McClanan, Jr.)

THE WITCHES OF PUNGO CELEBRATE HALLOWEEN

The early afternoon Halloween party at the Senior Resource Center on October 31, 2013, featured the Honorary Witches of Pungo, with ten of them seated at the head table. After the people present served themselves delicious refreshments, Rita Trammell, the coordinator of the event, gave a brief presentation about the life of Grace Sherwood, the Witch of Pungo. (*My previous books contain information about Grace Sherwood.*) Then, each of the Witches present told about their memories of the weekends they had served as the Witch of Pungo during the Pungo Strawberry Festival. Here is what they said:

Judy Cannon served at the twenty-ninth Festival. She saw it as a humbling experience, not something scary. She praised the fact that the Strawberry Festival is a non-alcohol event. Since she directs the Food Pantry at Charity United Methodist Church, which is close to her heart, she explained that the food pantry serves people who live in the Virginia Beach zip codes 23456 and 23457, and in Knotts Island, North Carolina. She thanked the Senior Resource Center for their support of this project through collecting donations of food items.

Anne Bright said that it is really quite an honor to be an Honorary Witch, although people who do not know the history of Grace Sherwood would not understand it that way. When someone asks how a person can become the Witch, she tells them that it is based on the contributions people make to the community. If you want to be an honorary witch, she said, you should get out and do something to help the community. This is not a cult, but rather a recognition of residents of the Pungo area who have helped to make this a better world -- not someone who is weird, with strange powers. The Witches are asked to help provide food each year for the Press Conference which comes before the Strawberry Festival, when the identity of the Witch of Pungo is revealed. (The name of the witch is usually a close-kept secret until that day.)

Joyce Salmons said that she enjoyed being asked to be the Witch. She grew up in Pungo Village and has always loved it. The Strawberry Festival "brings big time to a little community," she said. She is thankful that her father, Willard Whitehurst, was the Honorary Mayor of Pungo not many months before he passed away. He really appreciated that honor.

Jack Burroughs said ditto to all that had already been said. It has been a joy for her to meet so many nice people at the Pungo Strawberry Festivals throughout these thirty years. She is especially happy that the Strawberry Festival committee has given well over $500,000 to the community.

Betty Whitehurst explained that she came to Pungo as a newcomer in 1999, when she and I retired and we settled on the property where I was born and raised. She especially remembers when we rode in the convertible in the parade. Like politicians we waved and greeted people on each side of the street. Our chauffeur was a well-known Sheriff's Deputy, and whenever we stopped along the way people came over and greeted her. We thought that was delightful!

Mary Ellen Brinkley, the twenty-sixth Witch, is retired after teaching for many years at Creeds Elementary School. Her sister, JoAnne Stutzman, who was the thirteenth Witch, was the secretary at Creeds Elementary.

Julia Ogden was a long-time physical education assistant at Creeds Elementary School. When she was called to the principal's office to meet with the people who had come to ask her about being the Witch, she thought, "What have I done now to be in trouble?" She later got an award from the state for spending many years as a volunteer with the Rescue Squad – but her husband and her sons have always thought her highest honor was being the Witch of Pungo.

Paula Knight was the thirtieth Witch, in 2013. When Jack Burroughs and Anne Bright came to her door, she thought to herself, "I know what they are coming here for!" It was made clear she was not to tell her husband Barry, our Representative to the Virginia House of Delegates, about it. He only discovered the Witch was his wife at the Press Conference.

Becky Cullipher was raised in Pungo. She has always loved the Pungo Strawberry Festival. She remembers when her husband Louis was the Honorary Mayor of Pungo.

Robin Lee, the twenty-eighth Witch, works as secretary at Creeds Elementary School. She always comes to the Strawberry Festival, and remembers with a lot of joy when her mother Betty and father Floyd Waterfield were the Honorary Witch and Mayor of Pungo.

- - - - - - -

After a big round of applause, Rita Trammell recognized the two Honorary Mayors who were present and asked us to say a few words. Garland Eaton spoke first, and explained that it was a big honor to serve as Mayor. Then Rita asked me to speak. I remembered that when it was announced that Tim Lee was the Mayor, I said to Robin's father, "I see that Robin's husband Tim has on the same tie with strawberries on it which you had loaned to me when I was the Mayor." Floyd said, "It's a funny thing about that tie. One day I looked in my closet and saw that one of my two strawberry ties was missing. I wondered what happened to it. A few days later it was returned and the other one was missing." Robin had borrowed one tie for Tim to see, and then returned it and got the other one which Tim used. After I shared that, Robin said, "That was the only time I ever lied to my dad!"

- - - - - - -

Here is the list of the Honorary Witches of Pungo who have served at the Pungo Strawberry Festivals
(as provided by Anne Bright):

1984 - Jack Burroughs
1985 - Dorothy Whitehurst
1986 - Mable Brock
1987 - Rose Schnurbusch
1988 - Mary Cooper
1989 - Dorothy Dudley
1990 - Alice Flanagan
1991 - Lillie James
1992 - Patty Bonney
1993 - Faye Dorchester
1994 - Shirley Eaton
1995 - Joyce Salmons
1996 - JoAnne Stutzman
1997 - Ann Gregory
1998 - Anne Bright

1999 - Susan Flanagan
2000 - Bonnie White
2001 - Ann Henley
2002 - Becky Cullipher
2003 - Judy Doyle
2004 - Donna Vaughan
2005 - Debbie Keane
2006 - Nina Eaton
2007 - Julie Ogden
2008 - Betty Whitehurst
2009 - Mary Ellen Brinkley
2010 - Rita Joyner
2011 - Robin Lee
2012 - Judy Cannon
2013 - Paula Knight

Honorary Witches of Pungo (from left): Paula Knight, Julie Ogden, Mary Ellen Brinkley, Betty Whitehurst, Jack Burroughs, Joyce Salmons, Anne Bright, Judy Cannon (Not pictured: Becky Cullipher, Robin Lee.)
(Photo: © June Dunton Klag, 2013)

THE HONORARY WITCH OF PUNGO, 2013

In preparation for the Pungo Strawberry Festival on Memorial Day weekend each year, a press conference is held early in May. It is traditional to keep secret the names of the Honorary Mayor, First Lady, and Witch of Pungo until it is announced at the press conference. That tradition was very much in action for the May 9th press conference for the 2013 Pungo Strawberry Festival.

On that day, Paula Whitehurst Knight was introduced as the new Witch of Pungo, to the surprise of many persons present, including her husband, Barry Knight. She had been able to keep it a secret from him until the moment the announcer mentioned that she was the wife of a pig farmer. When she got out of the limousine, to the delight of the crowd, she was dressed like a witch in a black gown and a high pointed hat, carrying a broom and with a delightful smile on her face. Robin Davenport, the principal of Creeds Elementary School, was the Honorary Mayor of Pungo.

The custom is for the Witch and the Honorary Mayor of Pungo to meet at Herb and Carolyn Culpepper's Pungo Realty Office, across the street from the press conference, and put on their outfits in secret so that no one will see them prior to their official presentation. Since Paula's husband, Barry Knight, our Representative to the Virginia House of Delegates in Richmond, often stopped by that office, Carolyn feared that he might come by that morning. So she sent Herb over to the Press Conference to talk to Barry and try to keep him occupied at the conference. There was a large number of persons present and Herb could not locate Barry. So he did what was the next logical thing to do, and that was to use his cell phone to call Barry. When Barry answered the phone, it was obvious that the two of them were standing almost next to each other.

Nevertheless, the secret was well kept until just before the Witch stepped out of the limousine and was met by the applause of all present.

Before the event began, Betty and I had a small table, selling my three *Pungo Tales* books. I saw Ernestine Middleton, Barry Knight's mother and a good friend of mine since our high school days when she was a student at Kempsville High School, the rival of my school, Oceana High School. I told her that it was good to see her at the Press Conference. She responded, "I don't know why I was invited to it. I hardly know anybody here." I said, "Well, it's a good event and I'm glad you came." When it was announced that her daughter-in-law was the Honorary Witch of Pungo, it became obvious why Ernestine was invited. She was glad she came.

We never know what life has in store for us.
"Don't worry, be happy!"

A TRIBUTE TO FIVE BRAVE SURFMEN

My wife Betty and I attended the "Surfmen Memorial Service" at Tabernacle United Methodist Church on January 8, 2014, sponsored by the Old Coast Guard Station Museum on Atlantic Avenue, commemorating a tragic event that took place 127 years ago on that same date. The presence of a large number of uniformed Coast Guard men and women was evidence of the continuing presence of the Coast Guard in Pungo and the surrounding area.

Kathryn Fisher, the museum's Executive Director, gave words of welcome and an introduction. She said that a German ship, the *Elizabeth,* from Hamburg, Germany, had wrecked 12 miles below Cape Henry, halfway between the Dam Neck Mills and Little Island Life Saving Stations, in the midst of a snowstorm with strong northeasterly winds in the early morning of January 8, 1887.

When Abel Belanga, Keeper of the Little Island station, heard the alarm around midnight on January 7th, he jumped out of bed and joined other members of the Life Saving Service, including some from the Dam Neck Mills station, at the site of the wreck. After they tried repeatedly to toss a tow line to the wrecked ship, without success, Belanga ran back to the station, where he lived, to get the wooden surfboat and other equipment. He was in need of some breakfast, but it was not yet ready, so his wife served him a cup of cold coffee and a piece of pie, which he gulped down and then ran back to the beach to launch the boat. After he kissed his wife, he said, "The worst is yet to come!" That was the last time she saw him alive.

The ship's crew had gotten into their own lifeboat. About that time, a huge wave turned over both boats, and the entire crew of the *Elizabeth*, including Captain Halberstadt, drowned. Five of the seven surfmen attempting the rescue were also drowned: Abel Belanga, James Belanga, Joseph Spratly, John Land, and George Stone. (*At a history presentation at the Senior Resource Center in January 2014, led by Barbara Henley, I learned that George Stone was the father of Henry "Blind" Stone, the subject of one of the stories in my book,* Pungo Tales Three: People, Pets, Places.)

Only two of the 29 persons involved survived. Sadly, 22 German sailors and five American surfmen died. The survivors were Frank Tedford, a brother-in-law of Abel Belanga, and John Ethridge. The Belanga family was especially hard-hit; James Belanga was Abel's brother and Joseph Spratley was another brother-in-law. Marshall E. Belanga, who runs the Belanga Seafood store on Sandbridge Road, is the great-grandson of James E. Belanga. He and other descendants of the surfmen's families were introduced during the memorial service.

The widows and orphans of the five surfmen who died were paid what the men would have earned for the next two years. Funerals were held at Dam Neck and at Tabernacle United Methodist Church. Some of the surfmen were buried at Willowwood Cemetery across from Tabernacle Church and others at a cemetery on Pungo Ridge.

Mayor William D. Sessoms, Jr., was the next person to speak. He remembers in the past seeing ducks going from the boardwalk into the ocean. By "ducks" he was referring to "rescue boats." Mayor Sessoms said, "We must never forget our history. . . . It is important for us to keep Virginia Beach history alive. . . . It is fitting to have this memorial service here at Tabernacle Church because it was the Belanga family church."

Lieutenant Commander Ronaydee Marquez, Atlantic Area Prevention Staff, spoke next. She explained that the U.S. Life Saving Service began in 1878, and later merged with the Revenue Cutter System to become the U.S. Coast Guard in 1915. Prior to that, in the late 1880's there were five stations in Virginia Beach and Princess Anne County: Seatack (now the Old Coast Guard Station Museum), Cape Henry, Dam Neck, Little Island, and False Cape. The motto of Life Saving Stations was "You have to go out, but you don't have to come back." The emphasis today is making sure everyone comes back. A good example of that is the October 2013 rescue of two French Canadians whose ship began to sink near the Chesapeake Bay Bridge Tunnel due to cooperation between several lifesaving stations. None of the rescuers were lost. "What has not changed since the 1800's is the unfailing courage, outstanding leadership, trained initiative, and dedication to duty of those who serve in today's Coast Guard," she concluded.

Captain Paul Thomas, Chief of Staff, Fifth Coast Guard District, read the names of each of the surfmen who died in the 1887 incident. Lieutenant Scott McBride, External Affairs Officer, Fifth Coast Guard District, rang a bell as each name was read. Charlie Wiseman, music director at Tabernacle Church, played the organ as we stood and sang the Coast Guard Hymn.

After Rev. Jack Davis, Pastor of Tabernacle Church, said the benediction, a wreath laying ceremony took place across the road in the Willowwood Cemetery. Rev. Davis led the Invocation; Captain John Little, Commander, Coast Guard Sector Hampton Roads, and Captain Lonnie Harrison, Chief of Prevention, Fifth Coast Guard District, led the wreath laying; and Lieutenant Commander Ed Bass, Chaplain, Fifth Coast Guard District, pronounced the benediction. A reception followed in the church social hall.

Sadly, at the exact moment of the wreath laying, a Navy helicopter crashed into the ocean off Virginia Beach, not far from the site of the 1887 sinking of the German ship. Only two of the five-person crew survived, and the body of one of those who died was not found until divers were able to locate the downed helicopter with the deceased crewman still in the cockpit. Once again we were reminded of the importance of having the Coast Guard present in our community.

V.

IN THEIR

OWN WORDS

THE REMARKABLE JONES FAMILY
(Letters from Estelle Jones Bowers)

Estelle Bowers, who now lives in Goose Creek, South Carolina, wrote me two letters, one on July 15, 2013, and the other one on July 20, 2013. It is a joy for me to present excerpts from those letters.

My cousin, Hugh West, told me that you have written a third book about Pungo. My cousin's daughter, Edwina Stokes, who lives in Norfolk, purchased your Pungo 1 and Pungo 2 books and sent them to me and I am interested in purchasing your third 'Tales of Pungo' book. I was born and reared in Princess Anne and have strong connections to the area. In fact, I worked for the Rations Board and also was an airplane spotter during World War II. After I married and my husband was in the service, I worked as a clerk in the Court House.

I was surprised that you did not write about the Norfolk & Southern Railroad Company in any of your books. (*A story about that is in the book* Glimpses of Down-County History: Southern Princess Anne County, *compiled by Barbara Murden Henley.*) You did mention Guy Capps as being the 'Potato King' in one of your books. My mother, Etta Wood Jones, who was Goldie Bartee's oldest sister, was the agent for the Norfolk & Southern Railroad Company at the Court House Station from before she married until she retired. Mom was a remarkable woman for that time. She was the first woman in Princess Anne to work at a job other than school teacher or telephone operator – the only acceptable jobs for women then. She taught herself typing on her Underwood manual typewriter, and learned telegraphy because there was no telephone in the station and telegraphy was the only means of communication. I can still remember the passenger trains stopping there, as my mom took my brother and me with her to work. Mom also was the first lady to own an automobile in the county. . . .

When Mom lived in West Neck, she would walk to and from work, regardless of the weather. Upon arriving at the station, she would first build a fire in the cast iron stove using coal. After she married my father, Raymond Jones, he started working for the Norfolk & Southern Railroad Company as the agent at the Pungo Station. Each day he would use his hand-operated hand car to ride the rails from the Court House to Pungo. It was some time later that he owned his first car.

My brother Elliott and I grew up being at the station six days a week and would play across the tracks, or walk on the tracks or play in back of the station. As we got older, after school we would help Mom with work in the station. We learned the touch system for typing, as Mom put blank keys on top of the typewriter keys so we had to learn the correct way.

During the potato season, we would all help my dad at the Pungo station. There were times that we would only go home to bathe and change clothes. . . . Years later, there were no passenger trains, but packages and items were shipped by train as that was the only means of shipping until trucks were used and trains were not used any longer. One of my favorite memories was the ice plant that was across the tracks from the station at Pungo. I can almost hear its noise now! . . . .

My mother's older brother, Thomas Wood, was the agent at Munden Point Station for the Norfolk & Southern Railroad Company. . . . Uncle Tom, Aunt Helen, and Margery lived close to the railroad station. We used to go to see them often. In fact, Uncle Tom helped Mom learn the telegraph system which was used at the Norfolk & Southern railroad stations then. Uncle Tom knew, and was friends with, a lot of wealthy people who lived on Knotts Island or had second homes there.

. . . . .

I was born March 14, 1925, and while postage stamps cost $0.02 at the time, my earliest memory was when they were $0.03. Another memory was that my parents voted for Herbert Hoover, but I had a little kitten which I named Al Smith. I remember dressing Al Smith up in doll clothes and pushing him around in my doll carriage. . . . I have seen gasoline go from $0.25 a gallon to the present-day price of $3.50+ per gallon. I remember when we did not have indoor plumbing and got our drinking water from an outdoors pump. I also remember studying by kerosene lamps as a child. I remember unpaved roads and a time when we walked to the store and the post office instead of getting into a car to ride there. I remember not having paper products, such as paper towels, paper napkins, or toilet paper. (We used Sears Roebuck and Montgomery Ward catalog pages.) . . . I can remember the first sliced bread which cost $0.05 a loaf. . . .

When I was an infant, I became very ill. Mom and Dad took me into Norfolk to a specialist, and they found out that I was allergic to milk. With all that my mom had to do, she was told that she needed to boil oatmeal (made very thin), strain it and mix it with milk that every bit of the cream had been removed from. Dad bought a cow, and that formula is what I was given as an infant. My parents were never told about calcium supplements, if they were even known about 88 years ago, so I ended up with 38 broken and/or fractured bones, starting when I was in my 50's and until I moved here to South Carolina. My endocrinologist had me give myself daily injections for two years, and thank God, I haven't had a broken bone since. . . .

These are just a few of my memories growing up. . . . I do hope that I have not bored you with 'memories from my childhood.' "

I am grateful to Estelle for giving us an insight into life in the Pungo area in those days. My, how things have changed!

A MAN CLOSE TO GOD:
LONNIE LEE MURPHY, 1898-1995
(By Terry Gregory)

Lonnie Lee Murphy was my Sunday School teacher when I was in high school. I admired him very much for his deep Christian faith and his calm spirit. He was buried at the Charity United Methodist Church Cemetery on May 8, 1995. I had the privilege of being there for that service, and during the service Terry Gregory, his grandson, shared the following thoughts about his grandfather.

In 1898 the God of all creation saw fit to place on this earth Lonnie Lee Murphy. God had a plan for Lonnie and would love to bestow him with many of His unsearchable riches.

When Lonnie was yet a child, God said, "Lonnie, I need your mother with me. I've set up a home for you. I'll always be with you. I'll take care of you. Will you trust me?" Lonnie said, "Yes, Lord, I will trust you."

God said, "Lonnie, I have a wife for you. She is a good woman. She will honor and multiply your name. Together you will experience life with me. Will you trust me?" Lonnie said, "Yes, Lord." God said, "Come walk with me."

Time passed. God's plan involved six children and a home. God said, "I've prepared a heart for some money for you. Buy this property and this will be your land." Lonnie said, "Yes, Lord."

The walk continued. One day God said, "Lonnie, you have a son fighting in a war. I need him here with me." "Why, Lord?" Lonnie said. "Your ways are not my ways.

Only trust me," God said. "Yes, Lord," said Lonnie. "Lonnie, I'm calling another son home," God said. "Lord, I don't know if I can make it," Lonnie said. "Lean on me wholly," God said. "I will cause you to stand firm."

God continued to work in Lonnie's life. The family was now spanning five generations and Lonnie was a gentle, beaming head of a loving family. Lonnie acknowledged God as savior, giver of life, and God of love, goodness, and mercy.

One day when Lonnie was praying, he said, "Lord, my wife is weak." God said, "She'll be coming home soon. She has served you, Lonnie, for 71 years. She has delighted me." "My eyes are getting tired," Lonnie said. God said, "I have something left for you to do, Lonnie. Lean on me. Walk with me. Take my hand. Know that I am the Lord your God. I need you to be an example of wisdom for your entire family. Show them how to love. Teach them to be still and wait upon the Lord."

A few years passed and Lonnie prayed, "Lord, I would like to go home and see my land one more time. I want to smell the flowers and see the garden once again." God smiled, "Yes, Lonnie, let's go home."

During the night while Lonnie was home, God said, "You have heard my voice, you have obeyed my commandments, you have fed my sheep. Your seed is now many, Lonnie, come walk with me. Take my hand. Know that I am the Lord your God. Well done, my good and faithful servant." "Yes, Lord,' said Lonnie, "I will follow Thee."

MY PETS
(By Beth Swanner)

In my childhood memories there was a little all-white dog, with two brown paws. On Sundays, we would drive 100 miles to nowhere to get to Knotts Island, where Grandpa was a resident of Susie Litchfield's Nursing Home. He seemed so old and was bedridden, from a fall off his horse buggy in 1944. I was six and my brother was two. We would romp in the grass with Grandpa's dog Snyder, giggling as the pup licked our ears.

When Grandpa died, we inherited Snyder. We took him home with us to the farm and grew very fond of him. Sadly, he was hit by a car and we were deeply hurt when he died. I vowed to never love an animal again, so I would never have that heartache again.

When I was a child, we always had cats around the barn, but I ignored them and never thought of them as pets. But in 1972, my husband brought home a surprise -- a soft, white cottonball of a kitten. We named him Pepe. For two days he hid under the refrigerator. As he grew, a brown color appeared on his ears – "points" typical of a Siamese cat. His brown face mask was accented with bright blue eyes. He became a joy to the family.

Pepe developed a habit of desiring to go outdoors, usually around two a.m. He always woke me first. One day I complained to my husband, "Why am I always the one to get out of bed to let Pepe out?" He said, "Because he always calls for you. Notice how his sharp cry is ... "ma>>ma>>ma>>!"

Our last pet, "inherited" from my youngest son, Steve, was a sweet-natured golden retriever – a true retriever. If a neighbor left out a screwdriver or anything else, it could be found on our doorstep, as well as dead birds and mice. Steve bought the pup, naming her Sadie. One day he telephoned us that he was sick and that his dog had run away. We drove to his apartment and took him to be admitted to the hospital. We returned to his place to find Sadie in the back yard, so we brought her home with us, and yes, we fell in love with her. She was so full of love and more obedient than any child could be.

My husband really loved Sadie. She enjoyed swimming. We would take her to the pond and throw a stick or apple for her to fetch and bring back to us. One day my husband said, "Watch this," and threw a rock. When Sadie heard the splash she circled and searched and searched for it. We laughed because it sank and she couldn't find it. Then we threw in an apple and she was happy. She ran out of the water, shaking the wetness on us. Then she put the apple between her paws, sat beneath a shade tree and ate it all around the core, just as you and I would do.

Sadie was happy to go riding. My husband often told people not to get upset if they saw him riding around in his truck with another blond, because it would just be Sadie. As she grew older and was hurting from hip problems, if we asked, "Sadie, do you want to go bye-bye?" she would get all excited and hop around like a puppy. So naturally she had to go for a ride. My husband made a handicap ramp so she could walk up into the bed of the truck for her almost daily ride. We had her for ten years.

Once again I vowed to never love another animal. It was such a heartbreak to lose her. Now I have two stuffed, soft cuddly dogs. One is small and white. I call her Muffin and a brown one I call Max. They are nice to hug, they don't cost me anything to feed them, and I don't have to let them out or take them to the vet.

(Written March 1, 2006)

Six years later:

Now, there's also Stony – a cement dog that greets me at the back door with a basket of flowers in his mouth. He can't wag his tail, but there's a happy expression on his face. He was a Christmas gift from the "Love of my life," my husband Ishmael W. Swanner.

(Written October 21, 2012)

"GROWING OLDER IS PART OF GOD'S PLAN"
(A poem by Beth Swanner, presented at the Annual Senior Dinner, Church of Christ at Creeds, August 24, 2013)

        You can't "hold back the dawn"
        Or "stop the tides from flowing" . . .
        Or "keep a rose from withering"
        Or "still a wind that's blowing."
        And time cannot be halted
        In its swift and endless flight . . .

For He who sets our span of years and watches from
    above
Replaces youth and beauty with peace and truth and love;
And then our souls are privileged to see a "hidden
    treasure"
That in our youth escaped our eyes in our pursuit of
    pleasure,
  So birthdays are but blessings that open up the way
  To the everlasting beauty of God's eternal day.

Birthdays come and birthdays go, and with them comes the
    thought
Of all the happy memories that the passing years have brought
And looking back across the years it's a joy to reminisce,
For memory opens wide the door on a happy day like this.
And with a sweet nostalgia we longingly recall
The happy days of long ago that seem the best of all –
But time cannot be halted in its swift and endless flight
And age is sure to follow youth as Day comes after Night –
And once again it's proven that the restless brain of man
Is powerless to alter God's great unchanging plan.
But while your step grows slower and you grow tired, too,
The soul goes soaring upward to realms untouched and new,

For growing older only means the spirit grows serene
And we behold things with our souls that our eyes have never seen –
And birthdays are but gateways to eternal life above
Where God's children live forever in the beauty of His love.

www.ingramcontent.com/pod-product-compliance
Lightning Source LLC
Chambersburg PA
CBHW071145090426
42736CB00012B/2237